Banner Elk Breeze

By
Ed Robinson

Copyright 2018 by Ed Robinson

All rights reserved. No part of this work shall be reproduced in any manner without the written permission of the publisher.

Published by Leap of Faith Publications

This is a work of fiction. Any actual person or place mentioned is used fictitiously. Though some of my work is based on my real life experiences, most of it is a product of my imagination.

For my wife Kim Robinson, who not only condones my adventures but actively participates in them. Without her, I'd have few stories to tell.

Prelude

This is the first installment of a new series, *Mountain Breeze* - but actually, it is a continuation of the adventures of Meade Breeze. Our hero starred in eleven editions of the popular *Trawler Trash Series*, based in Florida and the Caribbean.

His fictional move to the mountains of North Carolina parallels my own relocation. I not only attempt to write what I know, but I also write what I live.

It is my hope that previous followers of Breeze will enjoy the new setting, and that new readers will go back and enjoy the first series.

Long Live Breeze!

ONE

Pop Sutton was dead. There was no doubt about it. The entry wound in his back was crisp and clean, about the size of my index finger. The exit wound was a mess of blood and tissue the size of my fist. His body was cold. He'd been dead for a while. He lay between his pot plants hidden high up on McGuire Mountain. I thought that Pop and I were the only people who knew of his little weed farm, but obviously, there was a third person.

Whoever it was, they'd decided that his crop was worth killing him for. I first met Pop quite by accident. Not long after Brody and I had moved to the mountains, I decided to explore my new turf. We traveled around the area finding waterfalls and hiking trails for a bit, but what I really wanted to do was get to know the mountain that we lived on. It was mostly wild, with only a half-dozen cabins scattered about. A lovely little creek ran through our property. Its source was high up the mountain. I decided to follow it, seeking its origin.

Brody didn't care to climb the steep rise or scramble through the brush, so I started out on my own. At times the undergrowth was too thick to be passable. I doubled back and hopped across the slick rocks to cross the creek in search of an alternate route. It was tough going. I'd been working on gaining my mountain legs and getting into better shape, but I wasn't prepared for the steepness and poor footing.

It took me most of the day to make it the three miles or so that I climbed. I was beyond exhausted and ready to turn back. The creek rose even further above me. I sat on a boulder to rest for a minute. That's when I saw the pot plants. Fifty or so scraggly green plants were spread in an irregular pattern on a semi-flat spot on the hillside. A thin overhead canopy shielded them from above but allowed enough light through for growth. There were no obvious trails in or out. I was still trying to comprehend what I was seeing when I felt the cold steel of a pistol barrel press against the back of my neck.

"You lost, mister?" a voice asked.

"I live here," I replied.

"I don't think so," the man said.

"Not here, exactly," I explained. "Down the mountain some. We just moved here a month ago."

"One of them cabins that Richard McGuire built?" he asked.

"Exactly," I told him. "The one directly next to the creek. I was following it to see where it came from."

I normally practiced a strong sense of awareness. I stayed vigilant, always studying my surroundings. It was a skill that had kept me alive during many troubled times. This man had managed to sneak up on me without my knowing he was there. I thought that I was alone in the higher reaches. I never saw a single sign that any man had ever stepped foot here until I stumbled onto the weed farm.

"Them folks down there usually mind their own," he said. "They ain't curious about the world outside their window. Tend to stick to the civilized attractions, ski resorts and such."

"I'm accustomed to being alone with nature," I said. "Just wanted to see what was up here."

"Well, it ain't a moonshine still," he said. "I wish you hadn't found it though."

"The name's Breeze," I said. "I happen to know a little about growing pot. I know a lot more about the distribution side. So I don't care if you raise some weed up here. It doesn't bother me a bit. Do your own thing, man."

He removed the weapon from my neck and took two steps back. I rose and turned to look at him. The gun was not in sight. He was a slight fellow, with a long mountain man beard full of gray. He stood maybe five-four. He wore dirty denim coveralls and a droopy brown hat made of an indistinguishable material. His fingernails were caked with dirt. His clothes were badly worn. He needed a good bath and a cheeseburger.

"The name's Pop Sutton," he said. "You may have heard of my daddy."

"Can't say that I have," I said. "You want to come with me back down the mountain? You're welcome to sit for dinner. Maybe clean up some."

"That's mighty neighborly of you mister," he said. "But I tend not to ask for charity from strangers, 'specially Yankees."

"Now, now," I said. "I took you pointing your gun at my head, but I won't tolerate being called a Yankee."

"Where ya from then?"

"Most recently, Florida," I told him. "Always below the Mason-Dixon Line."

"Well then maybe I can tolerate you living on my mountain," he declared.

"Your mountain?" I asked. "I thought it was the McGuire's mountain."

"Richard owns two-hundred acres next to where your cabin and them other ones is built," he said. "This up here's no man's land 'cept a man who can claim it. I done claimed it."

"You live up here somewhere?" I asked.

"That don't concern you," he answered. "But I know where you live, case the cops come a calling."

"I don't do cops," I told him. "I've been on the wrong side of the law enough to be shy of them."

"You some kinda outlaw?" he asked. "Come up here to hide from the law?"

"Not so much the law these days," I said. "But I've spent my time hiding from them."

"This is as good a place as any to keep a low profile," he said. "Hell, ain't too many folks even know I'm alive in these parts."

"It's getting late, Mr. Pop Sutton," I said. "I'd like to head back down the mountain if you don't mind. Your secret is my secret, and the offer of dinner still stands."

"You go ahead," he said. "I appreciate the gesture, but I don't associate much with people."

"I can understand that," I told him. "Is it okay if I poke around up here in the future? I'd really like to find the source of that creek."

"It's a nice little spot," he said. "Hard to get to. Real pretty view if you can find it."

"Maybe I'll cross paths with you again," I said. "Keep that pistol to yourself next time, okay?"

"I ain't no killer," he said. "I was just surprised to see someone up here."

"I mean no harm," I said. "I'm serious. You can go about your business without any worry about me."

"I'll hold you to your word, Mr. Breeze," he said. "Now go on fore it gets dark."

The climb back down was much easier, but I barely made it back to the cabin before sunset. Brody was concerned. I assured her that I was fine before telling her about meeting Pop Sutton.

"Do you think he lives in the woods up there somewhere?" she asked.

"He sure looked the part," I said. "But I can't imagine surviving the winter up here without good shelter and heat."

"Just like you to meet a character in the middle of nowhere," she said. "You have a way of attracting them."

"A weed growing, homeless hillbilly," I said. "That certainly qualifies as a character."

"You think he's anything to worry about?"

"No," I answered. "I promised I'd keep his operation a secret. I think we came to an agreement."

"So you didn't find the origin of the creek?" she asked.

"Nope," I said. "I guess it's further than I thought. It's tough going up that mountain too. I'll need to start earlier and take some supplies with me."

"I can put some power bars and bottled water in a backpack for you," she offered.

"You sure you don't want to tag along?"

"I'm happy right here," she said. "You can go play in the woods alone, mountain man."

I set out at the first hint of light the next morning. I moved faster than the day before, covering the now familiar ground. I made it to Pop's weed plants in two hours. There was no sign of him. I continued following the creek. My progress slowed as I picked my way through the brush. Occasionally, I had to venture away from the water to make it through. I could always hear the sound of rushing water, which helped keep me going in the right direction. Other than that, it was quiet on the mountain. No traffic sounds disturbed me. There was no air traffic in the sky above me. After four hours, I had to stop and take a break. My hamstrings burned and I was out of breath. I sat on a downed log and wiped the sweat from my forehead. Pop Sutton appeared like Scotty had beamed him down.

"I've seen drunk bears walk the woods quieter than you, boy," he said. "You done spooked every critter for a mile in every direction."

"I wasn't trying to be stealthy," I said.

"You gotta move smooth like smoke up here," he said. "You'll come across all sorts of wildlife if'n you stay quiet."

"I'll try to keep that in mind," I said. "You been following me?"

"I tracked you after you passed my crop," he said. "Figured you was looking for the spring that makes this creek."

"I am," I said. "Can't really say why. Just something I wanted to do."

"Since you made it this far, I'll tell you a little secret," he said. "You coulda drove your car to the White Rock Baptist Church and hiked about a half-mile to this very spot."

"Now you tell me," I said. "I'm only a half-mile from the road?"

"Give or take," he said.

"I didn't hear any cars go by," I said.

"The woods is thick and the creek drowns out the noise," he said. "Might hear a truck or a loud motorcycle now and then. Ain't much traffic up here as you know."

"How far to the spring?" I asked. "I'm about to run out of mountain."

"Another half-mile," he said. "But it's best to leave the creek for a bit. C'mon. I'll show you."

I followed him, trying to be quiet. We soon came to an open grassy area. The walking was much easier. I asked why there were no trees on this part of the mountain. He used a long stick to part some tall grass and pointed down. He exposed a flat stone with thinly etched markings. It was a tombstone. He continued poking with his stick and a few more stones appeared.

"Used to be the church cemetery," he said. "Bout two hundred years ago. Was a dirt track down the hill to what is now Pigeon Roost

Road. They brought pine boxes up here on a horse-drawn wagon."

We walked to the other end of the graveyard meadow before re-entering the woods. Pop wore some kind of soft shoe that looked more like cotton than leather. He made virtually no sound. He could duck branches, and bob and weave so as not to disturb the vegetation. I tried to mimic his movements. I had a lot to learn. When I stepped on a twig and made a loud cracking sound, he stopped in his tracks. He slowly turned to give me a look of disapproval. I was out of my element in the mountains. My world had been sand, water, and mangroves. I vowed to myself to learn the ways of the woods.

Finally, we arrived at a small pool surrounded by rock. There was no water running into the pool. A narrow channel in the rock fed the creek. It dropped steadily and widened until it resembled what ran by my cabin. The circle of rock and the pool of water held the trees back. The opening to the sky was almost a perfect circle. The sun shone down like a laser beam on the pool. It was midday now. Any other time of day and this phenomenon wouldn't exist.

"Good timing, greenhorn," Pop said. "Not many folks have ever laid eyes on this. Not recently, anyway."

"Thanks for humoring me," I said. "Just wow. This is awesome."

"Don't go running tours up here or nothing," he said. "This is between me and you."

"I'm honored," I said. "Really, thank you."

"Too cloudy most days anyhow," he said. "Especially during the winter months. You get this effect maybe a hundred times a year."

"You sure know a lot about this area," I said. "Grow up here?"

"Born and raised in Maggie Valley," he said. "Before my daddy moved us across the line to Cocke County, Tennessee, but I've been crawling around this mountain for years now."

"That's the second time you've mentioned your father," I said. "He must have been important to you."

"I wasn't very important to him," he said. "He was too busy sitting by a copper still or running the back roads with no lights."

"Moonshiner, huh?"

"You really ain't never heard of the great Popcorn Sutton?" he asked. "I thought everybody knew who he was."

"Popcorn?" I asked. "Is that how you got called Pop?"

"Daddy called me Little Pop all of my life," he said. "I hated it. I hated him for it. After he went and killed himself, I was older then, somebody called me Pop. I was so happy to be rid of Little Pop I just accepted it. Stuck with me ever since."

"What's your real name?"

"Marvin," he said. "Marvin Junior, but nobody ever called me that."

"Why did he kill himself?"

"Got busted one too many times running liquor," he said. "He was already on probation. Judge sentenced him to some actual jail time. He always said he'd kill himself before he went to jail. Kept his word on that score."

"How long ago was this?"

"March 2009," he said. "I've been hiding out up here since soon after he died."

"Moonshining in 2009?" I asked. "Not sure I get it."

"Folks think that anybody can just run to the liquor store and buy a bottle anytime they want," he explained. "I reckon that's true most places, but Cocke County remains a dry county to this day. So's half the surrounding counties. Driving an old beat up truck all the way to Boone costs more in gas than the bottle's worth. Plus daddy made good corn liquor. His shine was in demand."

"You never wanted to follow in his footsteps?" I asked.

"He wanted me to," he said. "But I never had a taste for it. Moonshining destroyed whatever little feeling of family we ever had. Daddy made himself famous with it. He was real proud of that. His celebrity status consumed him. He cared more about his legend than his own kin."

"So you decided to do your own thing, but shun society doing it."

"Something like that," he said. "Ain't fond of most people, like I told you."

"But you're talking to me," I said. "Helped me find the start of the creek."

"Can't have you trampling all over my part of the mountain unattended," he said. "It's in my interest to see you don't muck things up."

"How do you manage to survive up here?" I asked.

"I sell dope to survive," he said. "I don't need much. Most years I make enough to get me through."

"Most years?"

"Depends on the weather," he explained. "The soil up here is black gold. Thousands of years of mountain erosion and decay make it like Miracle Grow for dope. I got the creek to provide all the water I need if it doesn't rain enough. I'm hidden right nicely. Problem comes with the timing of the harvest."

"Short growing season?"

"Sometimes," he said. "The plants don't start budding out good until the equinox. Equal amount of day and night tells 'em to start producing good buds. The more time they get before the first frost, the better quality plant I get to take to market. The end buyer is real picky about quality. If the frost falls too early he don't pay much."

"What do you do then?"

"I scrounge what I can," he said. "I know which cabins are empty during the winter. I try to leave a light footprint. Most folks don't ever realize I took a couple cans of beans or an extra blanket out of the closet."

"What do you do for shelter?"

"I got a place to lay my head," he said. "The cold don't bother me much. It's the rain that gives me trouble."

"You know where I live," I told him. "If you ever get in a bind, you can call on me."

"I steer clear of Richard's part of the mountain," he said. "Don't need for him to know I'm up here."

"You got something against him?" I asked. "Or is it just disdain for people in general?"

"I got respect for the man," he said. "He done them cabins right. The one you got is hundred-year-old wood from this very mountain. He respected the land when he was building. Put 'em far enough apart so the neighbors won't bother each other. Found a way to blend them in with the landscape. He's a good man, but he's strictly law-abiding, a good citizen and all. He would not approve of my crop, nor my lifestyle."

"He's been a good neighbor so far," I said. "Nice enough to us flatlanders."

"He'd want to protect you from a dirt bag like me," he said.

"I see what you're saying," I said. "So let me get this straight. You live up here in the woods someplace, rarely have contact with other humans, make a good payday once per year, and nobody knows you're alive?"

"I got a sister down in town," he said. "I haul my load down to the road in burlap sacks. She picks them up and makes the deal for me. I give her a small cut. She only does it to keep me from asking for handouts the rest of the year. I done that a few times at first, but she don't have much and she shouldn't have to worry about feeding me too."

"So other than that you're totally independent?"

"As much as a man can be I figure," he said. "I take small game when I can. I can get my way into most of these cabins up here when necessary. I like to fish for trout but I ain't very good at it."

"I've been studying the creek since I got here," I told him. "Specifically looking for trout. It's not a good trout stream, but there's a few around if you know how to find them."

"Maybe you got a use to you after all," he said.

"I can catch a fish in a mud puddle," I said. "There was a time when I either caught a fish or went hungry."

"Alluding to your mysterious past again," he said. "If I cared what you done before I might be curious."

"There's only so many places a trout can tolerate," I said. "They want to stay out of the rushing water. They need a place to hide and wait for prey. Start with the deeper pools. Look for a bend in the stream or an overhang in the bank. Ambush points with still water. The good news is they haven't been fished. They're suckers for a dry fly if you can present it to them without being seen first."

"I ain't exactly got fly fishing gear," he said. "I got a stick with some line tied on it, hook on the end. I use grubs and worms."

"As quiet as you can walk these woods, you ought to be able to sneak up on them," I said. "Just let the bait float naturally in the current until it passes in front of the fish. Don't stay in one spot. Keep searching for those pools and likely hiding places."

"I been doing it all wrong then," he admitted. "I just sit on the bank and wait for a fish to swim by. Gets boring sometimes."

"Once a trout finds a good hideout, he doesn't move around," I said. "High water forces them downstream, otherwise they stay put."

"You have been studying the creek haven't you?" he said.

"I've got water and fish on the brain," I said. "I spent many summers fishing the Chesapeake, and years fishing Florida. Still adjusting to freshwater, but I'll master it."

"You made some good observations," he said. "Now translate that ability to the woods. Keep your ears and eyes wide open. Your sniffer too. Most city folks can't tell the difference between flowers and bear scat. I can tell you what kind of flower it is blindfolded. Same with the scat."

"Move like smoke," I said.

"Not in those boots," he said, pointing at my feet. "Too heavy, too rigid. Save them for the snow when you're shoveling your driveway."

I looked at his feet. What he wore was some type of moccasin. They looked homemade.

They were soft and pliant like slippers. They made no sound when he walked.

"Deer hide," he said. "Left the fur on but put it on the outside. They let my feet form to a rock or a log. Don't step on dry twigs. Don't leave a tread mark."

"Don't your feet get cold?"

"Socks is easy to come by," he said. "When it snows I don't move around. Can't help but leave tracks in the snow."

"You just hole up?"

"Snow don't get that deep here," he said. "Them ski resorts gotta make their own snow most of the time. Usually only last a few days when it does fall."

"I've got a lot to learn," I said.

"You seem sharp enough," he said. "But why do you care? You got a nice home down there. I'm sure you got all the modern conveniences. Why traipse around the woods?"

"I've spent the last decade moving from one adventure to the next," I said. "Most of them unintentional. I fed my wanderlust until I had my fill. The travel was never-ending. Now I'm putting down roots. I live on this mountain. No disrespect to you, but I want to make it mine. I want to know its ways. If I can feel its spirit, I can stay in touch with mine. If that makes any sense."

"We'll see how long that lasts," he said, chuckling. "You'll get tired of playing mountain man once winter sets in."

"You could be right," I said. "We'll see. I better get headed back down. It's been good hanging out with you today. Thanks for sharing some of your knowledge with a greenhorn."

"Come back with quieter shoes," he said. "Maybe bring some of them dry flies."

"How will I find you?"

"I'll find you, son," he said. "At least till you learn to move like smoke."

Two

Brody was full of questions when I finally made it back to the cabin. She was busy homemaking so she didn't mind me being gone all day. She had a nice country dinner going, something we never did when we lived on a boat.

"How did my mountain man make out in the woods today?" she asked.

"Apparently I'm a bumbling fool," I told her. "An embarrassment to nature."

"What happened?"

"Pop Sutton appeared out of nowhere," I said. "Said he'd been tracking me for miles. I never knew he was there."

"That's kind of spooky, don't you think?"

"He opened up a little today," I said. "Tried to teach me how to be a better steward of the woods. Passed on some mountain knowledge."

"Did you find the source of the creek?"

"Thanks to Pop's assistance," I said. "In exchange, I plan to teach him how to catch fish."

"Nice to see you making a friend," she said. "Even if he is a homeless, weed growing hillbilly."

"He's an interesting character," I said. "I offered him assistance or a hot meal but he refused."

"Maybe you can take him some food or something next time," she offered.

"I don't think he'd take it," I said. "I want to get him a cheap fly rod and some flies instead."

"Lots of fly fishing shops around here," she said.

"And I have to get different shoes," I said. "So I can walk like smoke."

"Walk like smoke?"

"It's how Pop describes his movements," I explained. "I can walk right behind him and never hear a sound. Meanwhile, I'm cracking twigs and kicking rocks. Scares off the wildlife apparently."

"Far cry from walking on a beach, huh?"

"I intend to master it," I said. "Maybe I'll start seeing some critters up there."

"We had turkeys in the yard this morning after you left," she said. "The deer were down here eating crabapples again. I saw a possum by the creek the other day. You can just sit here on the porch and see all kinds of wildlife."

"I'll do that too," I said. "But I still want to follow through on my lessons with Pop. At least until it gets too cold for me."

"Don't forget to split the rest of that wood," she reminded me. "Let's get it up on the porch so it can dry out before we need it."

"Yes, ma'am," I said. "A mountain man's work is never done."

I helped her with the dishes after dinner. We snuggled up on the couch and watched TV, also something we never did on the boat. I looked around at our little cabin. We had furniture, room to stretch out, a fireplace, and real showers. Brody had a whirlpool tub, washer and dryer, and a dishwasher. We had changed our lives so dramatically that it was hard to take it all in. I loved sitting out on the porch and watching the creek roll by. The water was clear and devoid of Red Tide, Blue-Green Algae, or dead fish. We'd given up our boat life to escape the toxic waters of southwest Florida. We'd also escaped any possibility of some anonymous bad guy finding us. There were any number of nefarious actors who may or may not want to take revenge on me for my actions. They couldn't find me here if they wanted to. I wasn't running anymore, or constantly looking over my shoulder.

Brody and I had shunned electronic devices in order to avoid someone tracking us. We did have a high-tech phone that was encrypted and allegedly impervious to hacking, but we left it turned off and hidden away. We made quick excursions into town for food and booze, but mostly we just hung out in our little hollow, enjoying our new cabin.

We drove down the mountain the next morning to Mast's General Store. They had a large shoe department full of fancy hiking shoes and boots. Everything was expensive. I asked a clerk for something affordable that would do the job.

"Out behind the store is our Little Red Schoolhouse," he said. "That's our outlet store. There are discontinued models and unsold stuff that's been discounted. Right now everything is fifty percent off."

Back outside we went to the Little Red Schoolhouse. They had tables, separated by size, of assorted leftover footwear. I found a nice pair of Merrell shoes for fifty bucks. They were light as a feather and extremely supple. They had an aggressive tread pattern, so I'd leave tracks, but I wasn't about to wear dear hide on my feet. I finished the purchase and we drove to the nearest fly shop in Boone. The salesman talked me into buying a nice five weight trout rod that broke down into four pieces. It came with a soft-sided carrying case. It was probably too nice to be giving to a homeless hermit, but I bought it anyway. I paired it with the cheapest reel they had in the store. Pop wouldn't need the latest technology to reel in twelve-inch trout.

Before I delivered the new fishing gear to Pop, I wanted to practice with my new shoes. Instead of walking up the mountain towards the pot farm, I climbed up towards the road, paralleling our driveway. It was steep and heavily wooded. I concentrated on careful placement of my feet. Instead of brushing branches out of my way, I ducked under them or dodged around them. I avoided dry sticks and twigs. I paused and listened frequently. It took an hour to cover the quarter-mile hill. I came to the road and stepped out into the sunlight. Just around the corner was a nice mountain view. I rested, catching my breath, and took in the scenery.

On the way back I crossed over my driveway and entered the woods on the neighboring property. The cabin owners there had dogs. If they heard me they would bark. I was trespassing in order to test my fledgling skills. I kept telling myself to move like smoke. I tried to make myself a human mist, wafting through the trees in silence. Halfway down the hill, I stepped on some dried leaves. I froze in my tracks, waiting for barking that didn't come. The sound of the creek must have drowned out the noise of my mistake. I doubled my concentration. I planned each step, keeping one eye on the ground below me and one eye on the low hanging branches in front of me. I made it to the bottom without alerting the hounds. It was a good first step, but I needed more practice.

I spent the next three days making similar excursions through the woods close to home. I split wood for a few hours each day and spent some quality time with Brody. I thought my absence might throw Pop off. It might give me an edge when I tried to sneak up on his turf. Finally, I was ready. I set out at first light for his part of the mountain. I went into silent mode immediately. I moved with stealth and purpose. My first encounter was with two raccoons. They were washing off apples in the creek and didn't hear me coming. I stopped and watched for a minute before moving on. I saw a few chipmunks and squirrels along the way. I spotted a red-tailed hawk on a high branch. The woods were now alive with creatures big and small.

I stopped and attempted to heighten my sense of smell. The odors ranged from decaying earth to wildflowers. I swear I thought I could smell wet fur, a deer maybe. I hoped it wasn't a bear. I hadn't seen any bears yet, but of course I'd been stumbling clumsily before now. I thought maybe I should carry a sidearm in the future. Pop had one, maybe for a reason.

Before I got anywhere near the weed plot, I slowed and tried to become invisible. *Like Smoke, Breeze.* I was confident in my silence. I hadn't screwed up on my approach. I knelt behind a fallen log and stayed still for a long time. I could feel my own heartbeat. I made a visual sweep of the opening where Pop's plants grew. There he was. He was wearing all gray and sitting with his back against a gray rock. He was motionless. I'd done it. I'd successfully snuck up on him, or at least I thought I had. Before I could make my presence known, he spoke.

"Not bad, greenhorn," he said. "You was good and quiet, but I smelled you coming."

I revealed myself and walked towards him.

"Not only are you wearing deodorant," he said. "But aftershave too."

"What? You didn't smell my new shoes?" I asked.

"Guessing you dirtied them up before coming up here," he said.

"Indeed I did," I admitted. "I've been practicing."

"A great improvement," he said. "But that fancy perfume you got on is a worse tell than your natural body odor. Nice freshly washed clothes is a dead giveaway too."

"So I should smell like dirt and B.O.?"

"Works for me, but I ain't got no shower facilities," he said.

"I brought you something," I said, handing him the fly rod.

He took it out of the case and assembled it. When he was done I handed him a little pouch full of dry flies. He gave me a long look and shook his head.

"I can't remember anyone doing such a nice thing," he said. "But I don't know how to cast or even tie these little buggers on the line."

"I'll teach you enough to get by," I said. "If you can tolerate my rookie ways."

"I think I can make an exception in your case," he said. "I see that you're trying to learn. Taking it seriously."

"Now I'm going to teach you how to catch a fish," I said.

First I showed him how to tie the fly on the line. We skipped the casting lessons. Instead, I stood alongside the creek, stripped some line out, and plopped the fly in the current. I let the creek do the work. It carried the fly downstream. When I ran out of line I let some more out. I handed the rod to Pop and he did as I had done. Before the fly drifted around a bend he reeled it back in. We walked the bank looking for likely trout hideouts.

"There, see that bathtub shaped pool?" I said. "The bank is washed out. Drift your fly in front of that hole."

He plopped the fly in the creek and stripped off some line. It floated temptingly downstream, but too far away from the target area.

"Next time use the rod to steer it closer," I instructed. "It's eight feet long. Get out on the rocks if you have to."

He nodded and tried a second time. The fly bobbed along in the current, approaching the cut-out in the side of the creek. I saw the swirl of a tail just as the fly disappeared.

"Set the hook," I called.

Pop brought the line tight and gave the rod a quick jerk. The trout flopped around in protest. I saw a smile on the hermit's face as he reeled in his catch. The fish was about fifteen inches long, a good eating size. After unhooking it, he placed it in a sack he carried on his side.

"Mighty fine teaching," he said. "And it's a nice rod. Sure beats a hickory stick. I'm much obliged for your kindness."

"You've got enough to increase your odds," I said. "Add a little more fish to your diet."

"I suppose I've played around enough for one day," he said. "I need to get some water on those plants."

"I'll give you a hand," I said.

We walked quietly back to the weed plot. Pop reached behind a rock and pulled out two makeshift leather bags. The seams were stitched together with rawhide. They were coated in some kind of grease. Each had a rope handle.

"Quieter than a bucket," he said. "And they hold up a lot longer."

"Those things hold water?"

"They leak a little bit," he said. "But if you don't dilly dally there's still plenty left."

We went over to the creek and filled our bags. I lifted mine by the handles and hurried back to the plants. The leaky seams dripped water on my feet, but I still had a good two gallons to irrigate some plants. Pop instructed me to put about a half-gallon on each plant.

"Put too much on them and it just runs off," he explained. "We'll let that soak in and come back around with more, later."

We returned to the creek and repeated the process until each plant had been serviced. Pop sat down and leaned on the same gray rock. He blended in perfectly. I was wearing blue jeans and a blue flannel shirt. I didn't blend in at all.

"Guess I ought to get some different clothes for up here," I said.

"Don't go buying no fancy camo shit," he said. "Maybe some khaki or light green for now. Brown when the leaves change. Leave it outside and let it stay dirty. Goodwill's probably got something that will suffice."

I felt a hint of satisfaction that my new friend had accepted my presence on his mountain. He wouldn't advise me on clothing choices if he didn't want me to come back. Maybe he was lonely. Maybe he could use an extra hand come harvest time. Whatever his motivation, I was glad to have another man to talk to. Over the past several years, I'd been with Brody and she'd been my only conversation partner. Before that, it was other women. Male friends were hard to come by, and I didn't often see the few I had. Now I was in a new place. The only other person I'd met was Richard, but we didn't visit or hang out.

Of course, we didn't talk about current events or sports or about most of the things two men always discuss. We talked about weather, fish, and the mountain. Pop told me a little about how he lived completely off the grid. He didn't let me know where he slept, but he described it to me. Early on he'd found a deep depression in the side of a hill. It had a rock overhang at the entrance, which was behind a tangled marl of rhododendrons. It wasn't as deep as a true cave, but he had slowly added vegetation in front of it to totally conceal its existence. He'd fastened a tarp on the ceiling to keep the drips off his bedroll. He caught the clean water runoff in a jug for drinking. When the creek ran calm and clear, he drank from it. Heavy rain muddied the water for a day or two, but he always had a reserve due to his tarp collection method.

Inside he had enough room to lie down and to store his meager belongings. He cooked with a cast iron skillet over a low fire, and only at night. That's why I never saw smoke up there. He had a sleeping bag, extra blankets, and some extra winter clothes. Now he had a fly rod. On rare trips to civilization, he'd bring back some paperbacks. Once he finished reading them, they became kindling to start his fires with. He liked regional stories about the Blue Ridge and Smokey Mountains. He also enjoyed reading the history of the area. He was well-versed on the legends and lore of North Carolina and Tennessee.

As I got to know more about him, I determined that his father's death had been the trigger for his ultimate escape and shunning of normal society. Even though they hadn't gotten along, something profound about his daddy's suicide drove him over the edge. I could understand. My wife's early death had caused me to snap. I too had run away from society. I'd hidden in the mangroves and back bays of Florida for almost a decade aboard an old boat. Even now, though my life was more civilized, I was on the fringes. Our cabin was our sanctuary now instead of a boat. I dreaded going to town for supplies. There were too many people in the real world, most of them assholes. Brody had attempted to temper my dislike of social settings, to little avail. Instead, she'd become more like me, content to be alone together. She jokingly blamed me for turning her into an antisocial homebody.

I continued my treks up the mountain to visit with Pop. Twice a week I'd find him, or he'd find me, and we'd go fishing, water his plants, or just sit and enjoy the day. I'd make these excursions in dirty clothes, not having showered, and using no deodorant. Pop always sensed me coming somehow. I worked hard on my smoke walk, hoping to one day catch him off guard.

Instead, the day came when I found him dead.

Three

I was high on a rugged mountain with a dead body and no cell phone. The coldness of Pop's body told me that the killer was likely long gone. The pot plants were untouched. They weren't ready for harvest yet. Someone would come for them before the first frost, or soon thereafter. Someone would probably come to check on them and give them water. I couldn't worry about that now. I'd have to deal with it later.

If I left him there to go down the mountain in order to notify the authorities, some predator would find him before the cops arrived. If I took him away, I'd be disturbing a crime scene. The pot plants would also incriminate Pop. I shouldn't have cared, but I didn't want the police to know that he was growing dope up here. I also wanted the plants to remain so

I would have a chance at identifying his killer. They were the bait.

On the other hand, carrying his literal dead weight down the mountain seemed impossible. I wasn't sure I could do it. *Think, Breeze.* I looked around me and assessed the situation. What I wanted to do was find the place the killer fired from, look for a shell casing or footprints. They'd used a high caliber rifle like a mountain deer hunter or bear hunter would carry. There were any number of vantage points nearby, but a longer shot might have been possible if Pop had been visible to the shooter from a distance. That didn't seem likely. Pop was careful. He was almost invisible until you were on top of him, but he would have known someone was there on his mountain before they got very close. I didn't have time to work out the dilemma.

I had to try to get him down the mountain and make up a story on the way. I knelt beside him and put one arm under his leg and his arm over my shoulder. I stood up, lifting him into a fireman's carry. I hefted him into a comfortable carrying position. He couldn't have weighed much over a hundred pounds. As I started my descent, I thought I could do it, but with each step he got heavier and heavier. I only made it five hundred yards before I had to put him down and rest.

I looked around again, studying the hillside. No shooters appeared. I spotted a thin fallen log and got an idea. I stripped the shoots and branches off it with my knife and looked around for another like it. Once I had two poles, I used Pop's jacket and my own shirt to fashion a drag sled for the body. I took his shoelaces to tie up the sides. I put him in the sling and lifted one end of the poles with both hands. I dragged him a few feet, turned around so the poles were behind me, and began a slow, steady march towards the cabin. I got jammed up a couple of times on rocks and roots but managed to clear the obstacles and continue downhill. My progress was slow. I tried to think what I would tell the police. I needed to keep them away from the dope, but not incriminate myself. I'd be their first suspect.

I wondered how competent they would be and how thoroughly they'd investigate. A good detective would see the drag marks and follow them back too close to the initial scene. There was probably some blood along the way too. My own footprints were all over the weed farm. Pop was a vagrant though. How hard would they work to solve his murder? No one would miss him, except maybe his sister.

I had his blood all over my filthy clothes. I hadn't showered in three days and my face sported a five-day stubble. They'd put me in cuffs the minute they saw me. I'd have to be evasive if they asked the right questions. I could always tell the truth and hope they overlooked my help on the weed farm, but my trust in justice wasn't strong. I still wasn't sure what to do when the cabin came into view. I stopped and put down the litter carrying Pop's body. It, too, was evidence. They'd know I moved his body, but I could explain that. Would they listen?

I knew I should be grieving the loss of my only friend, but I'd gotten tangled up in a preposterous event so quickly. I needed to work things through before I freaked Brody out with a corpse on her doorstep. I slowed my breathing and tried to concentrate. What did I know? There'd been a murder on my mountain. I reflexively wanted to solve that murder. In the process, I may have incriminated myself. The coming actions of law enforcement were unknown. Brody would be pissed. I was about to bring unwanted attention to our presence. Richard and the inhabitants of the other nearby cabins would be curious and suspicious.

Blood and gore had soaked the material holding Pop's body. It was a thick goo, quickly coagulating. I decided to let him lie there while I went the rest of the way to the cabin. I wouldn't leave him there overnight, but I was coming up with an idea. I removed his makeshift deer hide shoes and put my new hiking shoes on his feet. I put on his shoes. I walked in a circle around him to verify that I made no tracks. If and when they found my own footprints up at the weed farm, they'd assume they were Pop's.

I hustled the rest of the way down the hill to my front door. Brody was startled at my appearance.

"I'm okay, "I told her. "But Pop Sutton is dead."

"Holy shit, Breeze," she said. "What happened?"

"Somebody shot him clean through," I said. "Up at his pot farm. I've got his body. It's just up the hill."

"We've got to call the police," she said.

"Can't yet," I said. "I can't leave him up there, but there are some things I have to do first."

"What are you wearing on your feet?" she asked.

"Pop's homemade shoes," I said. "He's wearing mine."

"You traded shoes with a dead man?" she asked. "Son of a bitch, Breeze. We've been here a month and you've already gotten into some shit. I hoped that was all behind us."

I explained events as best I could remember. I told her what I was thinking when I made the choices that I'd made. There was no turning back now. She thought it over. She didn't yell.

She composed herself asked what I planned to do next.

"I'll claim I found him where he lies," I said. "I can sit with him until the cops arrive to protect the body. They'll search the general area instead of the pot farm. They won't find anything. But first I have to track back and make sure I erase any signs of my presence further up the hill. I need to clean up the real crime scene in case they ever find it. It's going to take a while."

"I hope you don't want me to guard him while you go back up the mountain," she said. "Not gonna happen."

"Okay," I said. "We'll wrap him up in something and put him in the garage. When I get done I'll put him back."

"You'll have to get cleaned up before we call the police," she said. "You look what I imagine a mountain murderer would look like."

"I need to get rid of these clothes too," I said. "Probably shouldn't go up there looking like this."

"Take them off by the fireplace," she instructed. "I'll burn them while you're gone and throw the ashes in the creek."

I got two big contractor bags and slipped them over Pop's body. I carried him down the hill and put him down on the garage floor. I spread oil dry all around him in case he leaked any more fluids. I cut the cloth from the litter and threw it in the fireplace before undressing and throwing my own clothes in. I took the two wooden poles I'd fashioned and laid them behind a pile of split wood further down the hill. I put on some new clothes before going outside to cut a leafy branch from a low tree to use as a broom. I grabbed a folding shovel from the garage and my sidearm from the house.

"Be careful, Breeze," she said. "I'll make my displeasure further known when you get back."

"Stay with me," I said. "I'll cover my tracks, put him back, and then we'll call the cops."

"I'm a bit worried about that," she said. "But I'm more worried about what you're going to do after."

"I'll identify the killer," I told her. "I'll collect the evidence to bring about his arrest and hopefully conviction."

"No killing," she said. "Promise me that."

"That is behind us now," I said. "No killing."

I wore Pop's shoes for my trip back up the mountain. I was in a hurry, but that didn't prevent me from moving like smoke. I was a ghost on a mission. I made it to the crime scene in record time, undetected. I shoveled up the blood-soaked earth and transferred it to the creek far from the weed plants. I used my natural broom to erase any trace of my presence. I carefully retraced my steps downhill, looking for blood spots and drag marks. I erased everything I found. I'm sure I missed a few things, but a random blood spot would be hard to find, especially for some investigator who had no idea where to look. I worked quickly, but quietly. The air was cool and the moon gave off good light. I was gone for hours. Brody was alone with a dead guy in the garage. She was pissed that I'd brought trouble to our door. I thought I was doing the right thing and it was too late now to change course. I'd removed evidence and tampered with a crime scene. I had to stick with my current plan.

I returned to the cabin and transferred Pop back to the new crime scene that I'd created. There wasn't enough blood on the ground, but I couldn't make him bleed anymore. It would have to do. I showered, shaved, and threw my second set of clothes in the fireplace. When they finished burning, Brody cleaned the firebox and disposed of the ashes. I built a new fire, to hide the fact that it was freshly cleaned. There was nothing more to do. We walked together to Richard's cabin and made the call. I returned to the body and waited for the police to show up.

They came slowly, with no lights or sirens. One car with two men crept down the driveway from the main road. Brody met them and directed them to me. They were deputies with the Watauga County Sheriff's Department. They each shone their oversized flashlights on poor old Pop. The lead guy was a big man with a big belly. He had thick arms and broad shoulders, like a high school football player gone to pot. His partner was smaller, thin but wiry. He acted nervously, like this might be his first dead body.

"You know the victim?" the big one asked.

"It's Pop Sutton," I told him. "Popcorn Sutton's son."

"I didn't know he was still alive," he said. "Or living around here."

"I ran into him a couple times, hiking by the creek," I said. "Don't know where he lives."

"He don't look like much of a hiker," he said. "Except for them hiking shoes."

"From what I could tell he was a bit of an eccentric," I said.

"Vagrant clothes, dirty, with hundred dollars shoes on," he said.

"I don't know much about him," I said. "Just met him in passing."

"Hear any gunshot?

"No, sir."

"What time did you find him?"

"Just a bit before we called you," I said. "Didn't have a phone. Had to run back down to the neighbors to make the call. Maybe an hour ago."

"You don't have a cell phone?"

"No, sir."

"No house phone, nothing?"

"That's right," I said. "We're up here to get away from it all."

"Until you stumbled across a dead man," he said. "We don't get much of this out here in the country."

"No offense or anything, officer," I said. "But does your department have a detective?"

"No point in trying to find much in the dark," he said. "I hate to say it but a dead vagrant isn't a high priority. Someone will be in touch. We'll get the meat wagon up here to take him off your hands."

"He's got a sister somewhere nearby," I said. "I think she may have helped him out occasionally."

"I'll look into that," he said. "Be good to have a next of kin. I'm going to have to get some ID from you folks too. Standard procedure. Won't bother you long."

"Would you men like a cup of coffee?" asked Brody. "I'll go start a fresh pot."

"Thank you, ma'am," the big one said.

He instructed his partner to stay with the body until the ambulance arrived. He came with us to the cabin and wrote down our information. I knew what would happen. My background check would raise some eyebrows down at the Sheriff's Department. Depending upon how deep they dug, Brody's history would sound some alarms as well. Our peaceful refuge was about to be invaded by nosey investigators.

Four

It took a while for the ambulance to arrive from Boone. There was no need to hurry. We were told the body would go to the morgue for examination by the Coroner's Office. The officers followed the ambulance up the driveway. We were alone.

"We're about to receive a bunch of unwanted attention," said Brody.

"Maybe I should have just left him up there," I said. "Not called anyone or done anything."

"I'm sure the killer was expecting the bears to clean up the evidence," she said. "They'll be surprised when they realize someone found the body."

"Which will make them extra cautious," I said. "Won't be easy to get the drop on them when they return."

"I want you to think about this long and hard," she said. "You can always just forget it ever happened. Ignore the weed and whoever comes for it. There will be enough scrutiny of us as it is."

"I know you never met him," I said. "But he was my friend. Up there when I found him, at that moment, I vowed to find his killer. I've got to follow through."

"Typical Breeze," she said. "Never leaves well enough alone."

"I suppose not," I said. "I can't bring him back, but I can bring somebody to justice."

"You just want a new adventure," she suggested. "Get that rush. Pump some adrenaline."

"Maybe so," I admitted. "But this is my mountain now. I can't turn my back on what happened."

"Fair enough," she said. "But we've got the law to deal with first. You'll have to wait until the initial excitement dies down."

"You're right," I said. "Let's see what tomorrow brings. We'll take it from there."

Tomorrow brought the big guns. The Watauga County Sheriff himself, along with the Deputy Director of the FBI. The Sheriff,

Tom Watts, introduced us to David Bowdich from the FBI. Brody knew him. They made some small talk before his phone rang. He stepped back outside to take the call. We talked freely in front of Watts.

"What do you know about him?" I asked. "What can we expect?"

"David has my respect," she said. "He started his career as a real cop, not a lawyer with a gun and badge like most of them. Moved up through SWAT. Made some real inroads into gang violence in California. Straight shooter. Follows the book. Takes no bullshit."

"Why do you think they sent him here?" I asked. "Sheriff?"

"I was curious about that myself," said Watts. "When we ran your records, Miss Brody here set off a red flag in Washington. The FBI has no jurisdiction in this case. No one crossed state lines in the commission of a felony. It's a local matter, but the Bureau insisted they send a man down. Never thought they'd send the top brass."

Brody had been an FBI agent. She was once assigned to track me down in Florida. I was on the run and determined not to be found.

After a shooting incident, she took an indefinite sabbatical. She used her free time to continue to hunt for me, even though I'd since been cleared and was no longer a wanted man. It bothered her that I'd escaped. She wanted to prove to herself that she could find me. She bought an old trawler and frequented my known haunts. She questioned people who might know me. Eventually, she succeeded. Her skill and persistence intrigued me. The twinkle in her eyes was irresistible. We fell in love and she never returned to her job in Washington.

We took off for a year and cruised the Caribbean. After we returned to Florida, the FBI called her to come to Washington. She was ordered to return to duty. Her refusal didn't sit well with the Director, Christopher Wray. We used all the political influence we could muster to put Wray in his place. He conceded the argument grudgingly. Someone in his circle put a hit out on Brody and me as her associate. Wray tried to stop it, but the assassin went underground.

We took him out when he attempted to ambush us at a marina in southwest Florida. The FBI had egg on its face and fell all over itself to make amends to us. We were never charged with a crime in the death of the assassin. It was all swept under the rug. The incident had a lot to do with us fleeing to the mountains. Now we were associated with another death. I started to understand why the Bureau would be suspicious.

Bowdich shook my hand with a firm grip and look directly into my eyes. I gripped his hand just as hard and returned his gaze.

"Mr. Breeze, right?" he asked.

"Just Breeze is fine," I said. "Nice to meet you."

"I won't bullshit around with you two," he said. "This just looks ugly. You show up here and immediately someone turns up dead on your property. Hell of a coincidence, don't you think?"

"We were just minding our own business," I told him. "It's why we came here. Not to be bothered by shit like this. We haven't socialized, made friends, or attended civic functions. Hell, we've only gone out to dinner once. We don't know a soul up here. We can't help it if some vagrant gets shot on our mountain."

"I got the impression that you knew the victim," he said. "You identified him to the Deputies that responded."

"Bumped into him up there," I said. "Exchanged pleasantries. He seemed harmless enough."

"What were you doing up there?"

"Hiking," I said. "Exploring the woods."

"And what were you doing, Brody?"

"I'm not really into hiking," she said. "I was here, baking bread or something. I never met the man."

"Aren't you guys going to investigate?" I asked. "He wasn't shot in my living room. You should be trying to find his killer, not harassing us."

"Our detectives are busy down in Boone," said Sheriff Watts. "I'll do some looking around if you can direct me to where you found him. They'll be up here later."

"I'll be standing by for a few days," said Bowdich. "Wait on the coroner's report and see what the detectives have to say. I have to ask you not to leave the area. I'll be in touch."

"On what authority?" asked Brody. "You can't interfere in their investigation. We don't plan to go anywhere, but why the strong arm?"

"Breeze found the body," he said. "If not a person of interest, he's at least a material witness."

"That would be for the Sheriff to decide," she said.

We all turned to look at Watts, who didn't like the position Bowdich was putting him in.

"Listen, Director," he said. "Whatever your interest in these two is, it likely has little or nothing to do with a dead homeless man. Unless we stumble onto a rifle cartridge or some other obvious evidence, we'll likely never know who the shooter is. We could get a warrant and search this cabin for a rifle if that's what you want, but I really have no reason to suspect Breeze of wrongdoing here. As he said, we didn't even know of his presence. Haven't heard a peep out of him or about him. We'll make an honest effort to solve the case, but I wouldn't get your hopes up. I have your contact information. I'll let you know if and when we have anything of interest."

"Thank you, Sheriff," said Bowdich. "But I'll stick around just the same. At least until I can see the initial findings."

"While not obligated to share any of this with you," said Watts. "I'll share out of professional courtesy. You'll know what we know."

"Thank you again, Sheriff."

Bowdich left and I took Watts up the hill to my manufactured crime scene. There was a now-dried blood stain on the grass where I'd positioned the body. The surrounding area was mostly rock. A morning dew had perked the grass up, concealing any trace of footprints. I examined the rocks carefully, looking for more blood or muddy tracks I may have left behind.

"This is one of the few open areas on this hill," said Watts. "Too many vantage points for a rifle. I can't see us tracking down the spot where the weapon was fired. At least not quickly."

"The shooter wasn't likely in the open," I said. "Probably set up on the edge of the woods."

"I'll leave that for the detectives," he said. "If they care to even look. This is the tiniest needle in a great big haystack."

"I'd offer to help but they probably don't want me bumbling around a crime scene," I said.

"They won't do much more than bumble themselves," he said. "They ain't exactly CSI."

"And there's no pressure to solve a bum's murder?"

"I hate to admit it," he said. "But this won't be a high priority. They'll go through the motions for less than a day."

"Which leaves me with a killer loose on my mountain," I said.

"Any idea why someone may have killed him?"

"Impossible to know," I said. "Maybe a poacher thought he was a deer?"

"If that's the case you might consider wearing blaze orange on your little hikes," he suggested.

He gave me a look that suggested he thought I knew more than I was letting on.

"I'll keep my eyes open, Sheriff," I said. "I'll let you know if I see anything out of the ordinary."

"You do that," he said. "Cooperate with my detectives when they get here. If you think of any details you may have left out, pass on that information to them."

"Will do."

"Nothing else I can accomplish here," he said. "But before I leave tell me why the FBI is here."

"Brody was an agent at one time," I said. "I was a suspect in my prior life."

"Tax evasion and embezzlement," he said. "Also a person of interest in a shooting in the Bahamas."

"I was cleared of that," I said. "Paid my debt on the rest of it."

"A man with a record like yours finds a body on his property," he said. "You can see why we might be curious."

"Brody and I have a history with the Bureau," I said. "They owed us a debt. Far as I'm concerned they've paid it, but I guess they're keeping tabs on us as a result."

"The FBI owed you?"

"Long story, Sheriff," I said. "Has nothing to do with whoever killed Pop Sutton."

"It does when I've got the damned Deputy Director of the FBI breathing down my neck."

"I don't want him here either," I said. "Trust me. I never wanted to see any of those G-men again."

"I suggest you satisfy his curiosity so he can go back to Washington," he said.

"I'll do my best," I said.

"Have a good afternoon," he said. "Wait for the detectives and give them your cooperation."

He left and I went back to talk to Brody. She was pacing the cabin floor, chewing on her nails.

"I've got half a mind to pack our bags and disappear," she said. "But I really love this place. Tell me it's going to be okay."

"It'll work out," I said. "Shit always works out."

"I'd like to know how you're going to get us out of this mess," she said.

"I'm going to find the killer," I said. "Take his picture. Hand feed evidence to our new friend the Sheriff, who doesn't seem much interested in solving the crime."

"Bowdich will pressure him," she said. "At least until he's sure we're innocent."

"We are innocent," I said.

"But you boogered up the crime scene," she said. "You tampered with evidence. Why did you have to do that?"

"We've been through this already," I said. "What's done is done. I'll make it right. I'll find the killer."

"When this is done you're going to sit right here and whittle doodads," she said. "No more missions. No more anything resembling trouble."

"Every time I promise that, the promise gets broken," I admitted. "I'm sorry for that, but..."

"But hell," she said. "Seriously, Breeze. We came here to put all the drama behind us."

"Our one and only squatting, homeless, hillbilly pot grower is deceased," I said. "I'm sure things will stay quiet once this is over. I mean, how much trouble can I get into up here?"

"I would have thought the same thing about living off-grid on a boat," she said. "But that didn't stop you."

"The number one reason I gave that up was to make you happy," I said. "That continues to be my purpose in life."

"Come here, you rogue," she said.

We had excitement of the wrong kind in our mountain hideaway, but it excited Brody in the right way. She pulled me into the bedroom and hurriedly undressed me.

"The detectives could be here any minute," I said.

"Then you best get a move on, mountain man."

I wasn't the type to object to this type of order from a pretty woman. It was quick but electric. Our current predicament was translated into a sexual energy that had to be satisfied. My newfound physicality made me feel more virile. I wasn't gentle this time. I was in charge. She asked for it and I gave it to her, good and hard. We lay there, spent, until we heard the sound of tires on gravel. The detectives had arrived.

I pulled my pants on and tried to button my shirt as I moved to answer the door. I figured it was obvious to the two men what I'd been up to. My face felt a little flushed as we exchanged introductions. Detective Ellis was accompanied by a technician, complete with camera and evidence collection kit. I closed the door behind me, giving Brody a chance to compose herself.

"I found him up there," I said, pointing to the clearing just up the hill. "I assume Watts filled you in."

"We're here to look for the needle in the haystack," Ellis said. "Have you been up there contaminating the site?"

"I just took the Sheriff up there," I said. "We didn't really poke around. Nothing much to see."

"Would have been better if we could have gotten here soon after you called it in," he said. "But that's police work in a rural area."

"I'll direct you to where I found the deceased," I said.

I walked up the hill once again, barefoot with a detective and technician in tow. They took a few pictures and stood there looking around.

"This is it?" asked Ellis. "Should be a lot more blood. There are no footprints, not even from the victim. Looks scrubbed."

"Don't ask me," I said. "This is exactly how I found it."

"I'm guessing the killer dropped the body here," he said. "Cleaned up afterward. This isn't the original crime scene."

"You're welcome to wander around the mountain," I said. "Lots of ground to cover on rugged terrain."

"Not really my specialty," he said. "I could ask for someone to consult, but I doubt my request would be granted."

"You mean like a hiking guide or something?"

"Bunch of them around," he said. "But civilians on the case brings up all sorts of chain of custody problems. If the victim was someone known to the local community you'd get a lot more attention."

"I got that impression from the Sheriff," I said. "So this is it? That's all you're going to do?"

"We simply don't have the time or manpower to do a forensic search of an entire mountain," he said. "It's an impossible undertaking."

"It's my mountain," I said. "I'll search the son of a bitch."

"I can't stop you," he said. "But if you find anything, you can't touch it. Call us and point it out. We'll take it from there if it indicates the real scene. In addition, one man is already dead. Keep that in mind."

"I'm well aware," I said. "I found his body on my property, remember?"

"I'm just trying to tell you to be careful," he said. "It may be your mountain, but someone's been up here with a high-powered rifle. Maybe this killing was just for killing's sake."

I knew better. Pop was killed for his marijuana crop. I knew where it was. I knew someone would come for it. That someone was the killer. Of this, I had no doubt. I walked the good-for-nothing detective and his tech back down to their car. He gave me his card and asked me to call him if anything else developed. I didn't bother telling him that I had no phone. I supposed I shouldn't have expected any different reaction from law enforcement.

No one cared about a man named Pop Sutton, except for me.

Five

Bowdich was back to bother us the following day. He wanted to talk without the Sheriff around. He was cordial and gentlemanly towards Brody, but I was certain he eyed me with disdain. He had sized me up and judged me unworthy. When he first knew her, she was an upstanding civil servant, dedicated to her job as a law enforcement officer. Since she'd met me, she'd turned her back on the FBI and walked a fine line between law-abiding and criminal. He blamed me for corrupting her.

"Listen, David," I said. "Brody absolutely had no part in this. She wasn't with me when I found the victim. She hasn't even been up the mountain. I don't care what you think of me, but she's not to be considered a suspect of any wrongdoing here. Let's get that straight right now."

"I don't know what happened here," he said. "But you know more than what you told the Sheriff. You have a history of entanglements where you've been loose with the law. Possession of marijuana with intent to distribute for example."

"I got probation," I said. "Worked it off."

"The shooting of a lawyer in the Bahamas," he said. "Whom you'd been previously involved with romantically."

He threw that in for Brody's benefit. It was an episode in my life she knew little about. When we first got together, we'd decided not to delve into each other's past relationships. Brody eyed me suspiciously.

"I was a person of interest only," I countered. "I was completely cleared of any connection to her death."

"But you were the one who found her body," he said. "Just like now. I guess you have a knack for being in the wrong place at the wrong time."

"She wasn't a body," I said. "She was alive. My actions saved her life, thank you very much."

"It is my belief that you know what happened that day," he said. "And that the truth hasn't been told."

"Your belief doesn't match the facts," I said. "I was exonerated."

"Now we have another body," he continued. "Shot through with a high caliber rifle round. Very little blood. No footprints. Scrubbed scene for a body drop, which just happened to be in your backyard."

"Maybe one of your Bureau buddies is trying to set me up," I suggested. "Settle an old score. Your people have come after me more than once and haven't gotten me for squat. Now you're offended that Brody chose me over your little G-man club. Exactly why are you here Bowdich?"

"You two want to just put your dicks here on the table?" asked Brody. "I'll get a ruler."

I saw her give him a look. Some non-verbal message was passed between them. She was good at that, but I thought I was the only one who could interpret them.

"Two things," said Bowdich. "Brody and I were a couple once. That explains my personal interest in her welfare."

"Her welfare is my responsibility now," I told him. "We're trying to make a new life here. We love each other. All we want is to be left alone, especially by the FBI."

"Here's the rest of the deal," he began. "We scrubbed any record of you two shooting that operator in Florida. We overrode local law enforcement and made it all disappear. We had no choice. We were responsible for him coming after you. However, if it got out that you killed again after we'd covered for you, it would be a disaster for the Bureau. We have a significant amount of liability here."

"We didn't kill anybody," I said. "I didn't kill anyone."

"But you know something you're not telling," he said. "I didn't get here by being naïve. Something went down here. Something happened that you either witnessed or are withholding evidence of."

It was my turn to get the look from Brody. She was influencing our conversation while barely speaking. She was telling me to be honest with him. I gave her a look back that said *are you sure?* She nodded in the affirmative. I had to trust her instincts. She knew this man well. I gave him the truth.

"Pop was growing weed high up the mountain," I began. "We were friends. I'd go up and visit with him a few times a week, even help tend to his crop. He taught me some things. I got him a fly rod and taught him to catch fish. He lived up there someplace. He never showed me where."

"Where did you find the body, Breeze?" he asked.

"At his pot farm," I said. "I didn't want the world to know what he was doing, but I want to use the weed to catch his killer. They'll come back for it."

"Why didn't you just call the local cops?" he asked. "Why'd you move him?"

"From what I see of the Sheriff's Department, they'd never make it up the mountain," I said. "If I left him to call for help, a bear or a big cat would rip him to shreds. I'd left footprints and maybe even fingerprints all over the place over the last few weeks. I figured I'd be implicated immediately."

"How do you figure you'll catch his killer?" he said. "Do you intend to stake out the scene twenty-four hours a day?"

"Obviously I can't do that," I said. "But Pop was one with the mountain. He was a stealthy mover. He'd been living there for years and no one knew. Whoever took him out had to be pretty good with his tactics. A rifle has a long range, but Pop would have seen them coming for a long way, or smelled them. He would have sensed they were on the mountain. The killer is a hunter or ex-military with extreme knowledge. He's also in the pot trade, or wants to be."

"Yet somehow you're going to be the one to catch him?"

"You won't understand this," I said. "But outside of Pop himself, I'm the best man for the job. I've been learning from him. I will find the bastard that shot him."

"And do what?"

"Identify him," I said. "Take his picture. Gather evidence, footprints and such. Feed it to the Sheriff. I live here. Who else is going to do it?"

"I'm inclined to believe your story," he said. "And I realize you have no sympathy for the FBI, with good cause, but this can't come back to bite us in the ass."

"Covering your ass isn't exactly a high priority for me," I said. "I just want to catch whoever killed my friend."

"Brody," he said. "If this goes south we need to know right away. Maybe you still have a sense of duty to the Bureau, enough to limit our exposure."

"We won't embarrass you, David," she said. "I think we've proven our capabilities."

He didn't want to accept that a lowly boat bum like me had beaten his best people more than once, but he begrudgingly agreed to let me do my thing. What choice did he have? He couldn't bring in a team to scour the mountain. Thanks to Brody, he couldn't pin anything on me. His hands were tied due to the past foul-ups of the FBI. He was on defense. He could only hope that Brody would keep me in line and protect the reputation of his employer.

He extended his hand and I took it. We didn't try to break each other's bones this time.

"Good luck up there," he said.

"Thanks."

Tension hung in the air after he left. I'd just learned that she and Bowdich were once lovers. She'd just learned that I'd had a fling with my lawyer. Both affairs were before Brody and I had ever met. They'd never been discussed, as per our earlier agreement. I figured that agreement was about to break down.

"Do we talk about it or leave it buried?" I asked.

"One shot deal," she said. "You tell me about this lady lawyer and I'll tell you about David."

I had a rich friend down in Florida. I first met Captain Fred in the Bahamas. I got busted with two pounds of dope and Fred arranged for my legal counsel.

"Her name was Taylor," I said. "She bribed a judge to get me probation. She used her connections with the Parole Board to get me the easiest community service in history."

"How serious was it?" she asked.

"It got hot and heavy for a while," I said. "Until she tried to live on the boat with me. We planned to run away to the islands together. She didn't last a week. It went downhill from there."

"Tell me about her getting shot in the Bahamas," she said. "You didn't do it, did you?"

"No," I said. "That was Holly. I covered for her."

Holly was my previous interest before meeting Brody. We'd spent years being off and on partners and sometimes lovers. The two women had met down in Belize. That episode of my life was safely behind me. We all wished each other well.

"So Holly shot Taylor," she said. "Was it some kind of jilted lover thing?"

"Taylor went off the deep end," I explained. "She was under investigation for bribery, not just in my case. She shot some poor sap and took his money and ran. She was with Captain Fred. I tracked the two of them down, more to warn Fred than to catch Taylor. She was about to shoot me when Holly took her out. I forced Holly to run. I stayed behind and got Taylor medical help. I was able to get through to Fred before I disappeared."

"And the FBI suspected you," she said. "That's understandable, don't you think?"

"I knew they would suspect me," I said. "Like I said, I was protecting Holly, who'd just saved my life."

"The tangled webs we weave," she said. "You've lived a complicated life, for an easy-going boat bum."

"Says the lady whose ex-lover shows up out the blue to keep tabs on us," I said. "The Deputy damn Director no less. They could have sent any field agent to find out what was going on."

"No they couldn't," she came back. "It had to be somebody we knew, or at least I knew. Someone with the power to pull strings. Our past is just that. Don't let it bother you."

"What happened between you two?"

"He was on the fast track," she said. "He really was a stellar agent. I could see that he was going places within the Bureau. I wasn't. He left me behind to pursue his goals."

"His loss," I said. "I think we can stop here. No point in picking at old scabs."

"Agreed," she said. "What's done is done."

We quickly changed the conversation, which I was glad for. We put our heads together to work on a plan to catch Pop's killer. She told me I needed a good camera, one with a telephoto lens. If I could get a clear photo we could present it to law enforcement. She asked about camouflage clothing. I didn't want it. I had my old dirty stuff. I didn't want to have to break in new clothes or get them dirtied up and left out in the weather. I'd keep the old stuff, and wear Pop's homemade shoes.

When would I expect them to return? It hadn't rained in days. The plants needed water. If the guy was a grower himself, he'd know that and be back soon. On the other hand, not much time had passed since the killing occurred. He'd probably not be in a rush to climb back up there. The side of the mountain where our cabin was built faced east, towards Boone. I knew that no one was using that side to get up over the ridge. That was my turf. He had to be coming in from the west, on the Banner Elk side. I doubted he walked from town. He'd have to find a place to park a vehicle. I remembered occasionally seeing trucks pulled off the side of Pigeon Roost Road. I figured someone was fishing. What kind of truck had I seen? I couldn't recall. I'd ignored situational awareness early after our move. It was time to turn it back on.

Brody asked how she could help. I didn't want her involved. She would be a liability in the woods.

"I need you here to feed me and fix my wounds," I told her. "Give me a warm place to sleep. Moral support."

"How are we going to communicate?"

"We won't," I said. "I can't be talking when I'm stalking."

"What if you get hurt?" she asked. "Or shot?"

"I'll have to drag my sorry ass downhill so you can fix me up," I said.

"I just don't like it," she said. "No backup. Help can't get to you. Hostile territory."

"Our killer is counting on all that," I said. "He thinks no one can track him or detect his movements. I'll prove him wrong."

"He managed to take out your friend," she said. "Who was supposedly a mountain man extraordinaire."

"He didn't have to get in close to make a shot with a rifle," I said. "I'll try to figure out where he fired from. Maybe find the bullet that passed through Pop."

"On a mountain?" she said. "It could be a mile away."

"I reckon the body slowed it down some," I said.

"Reckon?" she said. "Now you're talking like a hillbilly."

"When in Rome," I said. "Give me a chance. I'm going to try. If I come up with nothing so be it. Nothing lost."

"It will be a big loss for me if you get yourself killed up there," she said. "You keep that in mind."

"Yes, ma'am," I said, exaggerating a southern drawl.

Before moving to North Carolina, my best pair of shoes were flip-flops. I'd lost my good hiking shoes when they took Pop's body away. I had boots, but they were insufficient for a stealthy approach. I put on a pair of thick socks and the deer hide shoes. I gave them a test run around the yard. The fur outside was slippery. I learned that the trick was to use my feet like I wasn't wearing shoes at all. I practiced gripping rocks as I climbed around. On the plus side, they were incredibly soft and quiet.

A pair of khaki Dickie's work pants and a light brown shirt lay in a heap by the back door. They had cobwebs on them. I shook them out and changed right there in the driveway. A tan ball cap finished out my ensemble. A four-day stubble helped to darken my face. It all felt a little ridiculous. Should I rub charcoal under my eyes? Did I need random strips of burlap hanging from my clothes? Hell, maybe I could buy a ghillie suit like the snipers wore. I dismissed that train of thought. I'd been up and down this hill a dozen or more times, honing my skills. The only thing left to get was the right camera. That required a trip to Boone. I hated going down the mountain to town. The students of Appalachian State were back in town and the roads and stores were jammed packed. Brody was less affected by the mayhem, so I let her drive. I changed back into my civilian clothes before we left.

The traditional camera store is a dying thing. We did not locate one in Boone. We had to settle for Best Buy. The clerk who offered assistance knew no more about the choices than we did. We ended up picking the Nikon D500. It didn't have a true telephoto lens, but it would zoom to 80mm and it looked reasonably rugged. It came with a water-resistant case and a bunch of other goodies I didn't understand. It was compact and lightweight, which was a plus.

I wanted to play around with it once we got home, but we had no computer to download the pictures to. All I could do was look at them on the camera's small screen. Brody explained that it had a chip that we could take to the Sheriff. He could pop it in his computer and view whatever I got. That was good enough for me.

We ate a good meal that night and I got a good night's sleep. In the morning, I was ready for my first foray into the unknown. I was ready to hunt a killer. Brody fixed me breakfast and fretted over my plan of attack.

"Protect yourself first," she admonished. "The guy's got a rifle. He can take you out from a distance. You've got to adjust what you observe to compensate. He won't be behind the tree ten feet away."

"Good point," I said. "That will take some getting used to. I'm gonna go slow today. Work on long-range awareness. Might not even make it to the plants. That's a valuable insight, Brody. Thanks."

"Any doubt, any question, you bail out," she said. "You hear me?"

"Protect myself first," I said. "Got it."

I had a pistol on my hip and a camera over my shoulder. I was filthy dirty and smelled like a bear just awake from hibernation. I was wearing silly fur shoes. An image of Elmer Fudd came to mind. I told myself to be vewy, vewy quiet as I started up the mountain. Close to the creek, I moved from birch tree to birch tree, looking up and ahead. When I left the creek side, elms and hickories provided cover. Rhododendrons presented their own challenge. I liked to think of them as mountain mangroves. It made them seem more familiar to me. I kept reminding myself to look up and ahead as I crept through the underbrush. I opened all of my senses. I listened for odd sounds. I smelled the crisp mountain air. *Whoever you are, I'm coming for you.*

Six

I made better progress than expected. I'd picked my way over this ground enough times that looking up the mountain didn't deter me. I stopped about halfway to the weed plot and made myself as still as possible. I listened to the natural sounds around me, the occasional songbird and the light breeze disturbing leaves. I took in all of the smells of the forest, moss, and mud, the creek itself, evergreens and hardwoods. I could not detect the presence of another human being on this part of the mountainside.

I still had time to make it to the real crime scene so I pressed on. I maintained my awareness throughout the second half of the hike. There was still no indication of another person. I crouched down in some tall weeds where I could scan the area where Pop's pot grew. There was nobody home. I snuck around the perimeter to the opposite side and turned my attention downward. There was no one on that side either. Satisfied that I was alone, I went to the spot where I'd found the body of my friend. I studied firing lanes through the trees. I mentally positioned the body to determine the likely flight of the bullet. I doubted that old Pop had taken even one step before dropping to the ground.

There were two distinct possibilities, not far apart. Again I paused to use all of my senses. I detected nothing. The first option was two-hundred yards to the west, just where the woods thickened. There were several large rocks suitable for resting a rifle upon. I searched the place for any kind of clue. There was no spent shell casing. The weeds were trampled and there were no obvious footprints. I moved on to the second possibility. It wasn't quite as far from the body, had the clearer of the two firing lanes, but was less concealed. A man would likely have to already be set up in position when Pop arrived, otherwise he would have been detected.

I didn't find footprints, but the earth was disturbed on the backside of a boulder, like the prints had been brushed away. It hadn't rained here since the event. I knelt down and studied everything closely. I found a patch of moss on the boulder that could have shown the outline of an arm resting, pointing a rifle. A few weeds were snapped off unnaturally, something Pop wouldn't have done. I was pretty sure this was where the shot came from. Still no shell casing, though.

I stood up and looked towards where Pop's body had been. I went around behind the boulder and lined up the shot with an imaginary weapon. Where would the bullet go? Unless it lodged in a tree it would have gone way out over the ridge and arced into the valley below. I found myself concentrating too much on the scene. I couldn't afford to let my guard down. I crept back to my original vantage point and concealed myself in the brush. I refocused my senses. As my heart rate slowed, the sights, sounds, and smells amplified. At that moment, I was transformed. I understood how Pop had done it. My senses had evolved to a higher dimension.

I could hear a worm crawling. I could differentiate dozens of aromas. My vision was amazingly keen. It was all very spiritual rather than physical. I'd never been a very spiritual man, but here on this mountaintop, I was becoming more than myself. I was living elevated, taking in all the signals that nature provided like never before.

All the various stimuli bombarding my senses threatened to overwhelm me. I was acutely aware that I was still alone, but I feared I'd get lost in this new world. I managed to dial it back a few notches. I regained control while still experiencing the sensation of heightened senses. I retraced my earlier steps. The man had knelt behind a boulder and propped his weapon there before firing. He left little trace during his approach but had obviously attempted to cover up around his shooting platform. He had not walked over to his kill. He'd left the way he came, after picking up the used shell casing.

I looked back behind me, visualizing the path of the bullet. It was possible that it wound up in a tree trunk, but a few inches, either way, made the difference. It would take too much time to search for it that day. I was running out of daylight. Brody would have a fit if I lingered long after dark. I clicked off a bunch of pictures with the camera to jog my memory later. So far I had nothing but my intuition to go on. I knew what had happened, in my mind, but it was far from provable. I called it a day and started towards home.

Halfway down I stopped and tried to regain that enlightened state of consciousness I'd experienced earlier. I rested so that my heart rate would slow. I breathed in slow and deep, relaxing. I opened my mind to accept this new phenomenon. It came back slowly, first the sounds, then the smells. When I realized that my eyesight had sharpened dramatically, I knew I was able to harness this capability. I also knew that it would serve me well as I hunted Pop's killer. I would need it if I wanted to survive. I thought about how foolish I'd been thinking that I was capable enough. I'd had no idea just how good Pop must have been at it, but somehow he was able to show me how it was done even after his death. I saw no ghosts, but I felt his presence. He gave me an approving smile from somewhere in the cosmos.

I continued down the mountain, plotting my next moves. I needed to approach the site from the west next time. I wanted to look for traces of the man, try to figure out where he was starting his climb. I would check the road daily for a truck parked in a conspicuous place. I'd take note of trucks in driveways that I could see from the road, look for ones that didn't belong. I thought about the timing of this thing. Those plants needed water soon. He had to come. How was I going to be there at the right time? Should I carry a pack and plan on camping out for a few days? I doubted Brody would approve.

The descent was a quick one. I wasn't worried about being watched. No one was there to detect me. I was still quiet, but my improving skills let me slide through the woods at a good clip without making noise. The outside light was on at the cabin already, even though it wasn't fully dark. I could smell dinner cooking from fifty yards away. I was hungry, but not tired. I felt energized by the day's experience. Yes, I'd been naïve at first, but now I knew that I could do this. Besides, it wasn't a fight to the death. All I needed to do was get the man's picture to the Sheriff and create a plausible scenario for them to arrest him. It would come together.

Brody was in the kitchen. She looked as lovely as the food smelled. I, on the other hand, looked like a homeless person with no care towards personal hygiene.

"Straight to the shower, mountain man," she demanded. "We'll talk after."

I obeyed her command. I was indeed ripe. It didn't bother me up in the hills, but inside the cabin, I knew I was just plain disgusting. I stepped outside the back door and shed my clothes, leaving them in a heap by the steps. I walked back through the cabin to the bathroom naked, embarrassed by how stinky I really was. I ran the hot water for several minutes before stepping into the shower. Our cabin had an interesting water system. There was no pump for the house. Higher up on the mountain was a well and a thousand-gallon water tank. The pump kept the tank full at all times, but the house was fed by gravity only. The water ran downhill to the cabin. The big advantage of such a system was that we'd still have hot water when the power went out. The disadvantage was the lack of decent water pressure. The shower dribbled out water. At least it was good and hot. I stood there and slowly turned. I had days worth of caked on dirt to remove. Once clean, I had a serious stubble to scrape off my face. I'd done my mountain thing, now I needed to do my Brody thing.

I was clean, but I skipped the deodorant and aftershave. I'd need a day to lose the scent of the soap and shampoo. I presented myself back in the kitchen.

"I'm clean," I said, spinning around for inspection.

"Excellent," she replied. "Now sit down and eat. Tell me all about it."

I told her about my day. I told her I knew where the shot had been fired from. I thought I knew from what direction the killer came up the hill. I could replay the scene in my mind. She followed along dutifully until I tried to explain my newfound ability to heighten my senses.

"You're jerking me around, right?" she said. "Did you get bit by a radioactive spider or something?"

"I'm not kidding," I said. "It feels completely normal. Like communing with nature."

"Maybe you should take a few days off," she suggested. "Come back to earth."

"I will unless I see something that tells me I need to get back up there," I said. "I want to patrol the road down to Banner Elk. Try to spot where he starts his hike."

"It's two miles down to 194," she said. "What do you mean patrol?"

"I'm thinking he parks his truck along there someplace," I said. "Climbs up the shortest route or the easiest."

"Okay, I've seen a truck or two off the road," she said. "There are only two or three likely spots."

"Add the church," I said. "And friends' driveways."

"By the time you flag a truck," she said. "He might already be up there."

"Good point," I said. "Doesn't mean I can't get to him before he comes back down."

"Good lord," she said. "I don't like the sound of that. You need to be prepared."

"So I'll have to stay prepared until it's time," I said. "Sooner or later I'm going to have to stake him out. Wait for him, maybe over a few days."

"You want to sleep up there?"

"I'll be fine at night," I said. "He won't come in the dark."

"What about bears?"

"I haven't seen one yet," I said. "Pop spent years living up there. Bears didn't bother him."

"This isn't Florida, Breeze," she said. "You aren't on your natural turf. Are you sure you want to carry through with this?"

"I feel like I can do it," I told her. "You haven't been up there with me. No offense, but you just don't understand the transformation I've been going through. I like it here, living on dirt. Today I felt one thousand percent in touch with my surroundings… like I belonged."

"I'm not sure I'm buying this whole super sensory perception claim," she said. "It sounds weird."

"Let me try to explain," I said. "You and I both have always practiced discipline when it comes to awareness, right? We have an above normal ability to recognize what's going on around us. We can spot anomalies, things out of place. We can size up people. We're always one step ahead of what's about to happen."

"I was trained to do that," she said. "It seems to come naturally to you."

"Let's extend that another step," I said. "When we're underway on the boat I can sense things. I hear the sound of the engine, feel the movement of the waves. I gauge the speed of the current and the phase of the tide. I was one with the boat and the sea."

"I always considered that your gift," she said. "You were born to it."

"I've simply transferred that innate ability to my new surroundings," I said.

"Just like that?"

"With Pop's help," I said. "In his own way, he instructed me how to be open to it. He must have sensed my capabilities."

"Doesn't sound so unreasonable now," she said. "I think I get it. I just haven't been sharing that part of our new life with you."

"I'd love it if you would," I said. "But now is not the time. Let me take care of this myself. When it's over, you can join me."

"I think I'd like that," she said. "Mountain Brody."

"Mountain Breeze," I said. "Welcome home, baby."

Seven

I was up early the next morning. Before I even got my coffee I drove the length of Pigeon Roost Road. No odd trucks were spotted. I turned right on 194 and circled back towards home. I quietly slipped back into the house and poured a cup of black goodness. I sat on the porch and watched a doe eat apples out of the creek. Have you ever seen a deer bob for apples? Hummingbirds alternated at the feeder Brody had hung. Something had eaten all the bird seed overnight, probably squirrels. I was behind on my wood splitting duties. I skipped the morning shower.

Brody appeared in her robe, asking if I'd like her to cook breakfast. She wasn't part of the advance team, but she did a hell of a job with support. I appreciated her patience with my shenanigans. I wasn't sure how far I could push it though. I decided to take care of some chores at the cabin. I needed to bring in more wood and the ax needed sharpening. I'd drive the road a few more times throughout the day. In my bones, I knew the killer would be appearing at the weed patch soon. He could avoid tending the plants if we got a good rain, but none was forecast. The woods were dry. Even the creek was at a low ebb.

After breakfast, I tended to my duties, but my mind was elsewhere. All I could think about was capturing a killer, getting his face on camera. I'd also developed a likely backstory to tell the Sheriff. Pop got himself killed by stumbling onto the weed farm. Pictures and video of the guy watering the plants would be incriminating. He didn't need a body lying in his workspace, so he dumped it near my cabin, cleaned up the mess later. The evidence against him would be overwhelming. His only defense would be that he shot Pop in order to steal the weed. That it wasn't originally planted by him. I doubted that would fly in court. The defendant would be in a bad spot.

I drove the road again before dinner. I saw no trucks that looked out of place, but I did find something else. On a steep hillside, there was a grass track drive up into the woods. It wasn't more than a trail, but the grass had been beaten down by tires over the years. A four-wheel-drive vehicle would be required to navigate it. It would be unpassable in bad weather no matter the truck or its tires. I'd seen it before but paid it no mind. I guessed it led to a hunting camp. No permanent residence would have such a rudimentary driveway. It wasn't far from the White Rock Baptist Church. Pop had told me about the possible shortcut on this side of the mountain. It had to be the killer's access point.

I went home and told Brody what I planned to do, hoping she wouldn't force me to abandon my plans.

"I'll get prepared tonight," I told her. "You can drop me off at that grass trail. I'll ascend the mountain from the Banner Elk side instead of from here. I'll look for trails or signs of the guy."

"What happens when you get up there?" she asked. "What are you going to do if he isn't there or doesn't show up?"

"I'll wait for him," I said. "I'll bed down up there for a night or two. He'll show soon."

"I knew it would come to this," she said. "I'll be fine here, but I'll worry myself nuts about you up there."

"I'll be armed," I began. "I'll have some food and water. I'll find or make a shelter. I can do this Brody."

"You realize you're not thirty anymore, right?" she said. "We're supposed to be slowing down. Enjoying a stress-free life."

"I'll admit I was feeling my age when we left Florida," I said. "I don't know if it was the heat, the Red Tide, or what. I was starting to feel old down there, but now I'm reinvigorated. I'm getting good exercise. My appetite is better. The air is clean and crisp. My joints don't hurt and I sleep much better. Maybe I don't feel like I'm thirty, but I feel as good as I have in years."

"I've been noticing that too," she said. "I can breathe up here. I look forward to a new day. I've got room to move around in this house, not like on the boat."

"Do you miss it?" I asked.

"Do you?" she countered.

"I thought I would but I don't," I said. "I don't look back. I'm loving it here. That was one episode in our lives. It was a good one, but we're beginning a new episode now."

"I thought I'd miss the beach or even the pool at the marina," she said. "I don't even think about it now. I do want to start hiking with you though, when things settle down."

"I'd enjoy that," I said. "I know you'll love it. There are hundreds of waterfalls around here."

"I'll make a list and we'll see them all," she said. "Do you want to do that Banner Elk Vineyard tour soon?"

"Sure," I said. "I'll even suffer through the antique shops with you if you want."

After dinner, Brody cleaned and checked my pistol. I'd upgraded from my old 9mm to a .40 Smith & Wesson, mostly due to the possibility of a bear encounter. She was our weapons expert and a crack shot. I was not a good shot when we first met. I was never really a handgun or rifle guy. My trusty shotgun had served me well enough over the years. She taught me patiently until I was pretty decent with a handgun. I loaded a backpack with water, power bars, and some jerky. I couldn't carry too much weight. I had the gun and camera to deal with too.

I put all of the gear outside and covered it with my dirty mountain clothes. I went to bed early, planning on a full night's sleep, but Brody had other ideas. This time she took charge. I gave in to her, not that I had a choice. It was nice to be taken care of sometimes. It also put me to sleep in short order. *Thanks, Brody.*

I was up before dawn, anxious to get the expedition underway. Brody was still asleep and I hated to wake her. I took my coffee to the porch and listened to the sound of the creek. Sunsets here were obscured by the tall trees, but I enjoyed the quiet stillness of the morning. I noticed the fullness of the apple trees and the abundance of fruit on the ground beneath them. The deer would be happy about that. I saw that a few trees had already begun to change color, even though it was still August. My surroundings were already beautiful, but I bet they'd become spectacular in the Fall.

Brody came out already dressed. She gave me a nod that said *are you ready*? I nodded back.

"Let's do this, mountain man," she said. "I'll hold the fort while you're gone. Come back in one piece."

"That's the plan," I said. "Try not to worry too much."

She drove us up McGuire Mountain Road and turned left on Pigeon Roost. The road wound back and forth sharply for the first mile. I motioned for her to slow down before we reached the grass drive I was looking for. I rolled my window down to listen for approaching cars. She stopped and I got out quickly and closed the door. I waved her on. She disappeared down the hill and I hustled away from the road and up the trail.

I climbed two hundred feet before stopping. I was out of sight from the road below. There were no fresh tire tracks. I hadn't missed my man. I eyed the woods on either side of the trail. If a truck did start climbing the hill, I'd need a place to get out of sight. The brush on both sides was thick. I'd have to bash through it to gain concealment, and that would leave a sign. There was nothing else I could do. Hopefully, the driver would miss it or think a deer had come through.

I continued the uphill climb until the land leveled out. What I found didn't qualify as a cabin. It was more of a shack. It was roughly twenty by twenty square. There was a stout padlock on the door and thick curtains in the windows. A galvanized smokestack poked through the roof. Piles of split and un-split wood were scattered about. Empty beer cans littered the ground along with the occasional liquor bottle. The wood plank siding was gray and weathered. The tin roof was covered in pine needles and looked to have seen better days.

Behind the shack, I found a wooden block and tackle with old blood pools beneath it. That's where they hung deer to bleed out in the winter time. Near that was a small structure that may have been an outhouse. I looked for power lines leading to the shack but saw none. One of the hunters that used this shack must have discovered Pop's weed patch by random chance. He saw an opportunity and took it. The harvest could easily be distributed from this home base. No one would see a thing.

I remembered the camera and took some pictures of the crude structure. Then I thought of a question that a defense lawyer might have. Why would someone haul a body down the opposite side of the mountain in order to dump it near my place? It would be a lot of unnecessary effort. They could have disposed of it anywhere on their way back to camp, let the bears get to it. They could have buried it here on site. They could have dumped it near some other houses close the Baptist Church.

These were good points, but a competent prosecutor should have some plausible explanation. If he was local, he may not have wanted to implicate folks he knew that lived near the camp. He didn't know the outsiders who'd bought from Richard McGuire. They were probably transplants from the city that he despised. This was a detail for later contemplation. All I could do was identify the suspect. The rest would play out on its own.

I'd gathered all the information that I could from the shack. I began my trek upward. There were several clear trails leading away from the camp. I got my bearings and chose the most likely one. It soon deteriorated and gave way to wilderness. Deer hunting should be good over here. The camp was just a place to stage and drink beer later. No one would spend much time there. Who wants to be without electricity and poop in a hole?

As I put some distance between myself and the shack, I dialed up my awareness level. I was positive no one was out in front of me. I was certain that the shack was where my quarry would begin his ascent. I was ahead of him. I'd left no trace that I'd been there or anywhere along the trail. I felt good about the situation. He'd come later today or tomorrow. The plants needed water. He couldn't be so dumb as to not realize that. The crop was his cash cow. He'd take care of it or his murderous act would be for nothing.

I didn't think I needed it yet, so I didn't go into full-blown alert mode during the rest of the trip. I was aware. I listened and smelled and closely observed, but reserved my super keen sensory perception for when it was absolutely necessary. Occasionally I stopped and listened for sounds from below. I looked up for a man with a rifle. I listened for a truck or an ATV but heard none. It was a much shorter hike from this side of the mountain to the weed farm. I arrived before noon.

I sat and observed from the perimeter for twenty minutes. Nothing had changed. No one had been up here since my last visit. I went to the boulder where I believed the shot was fired from. I looked back again at where I'd found the body. I felt like I had some time to look for the bullet. It was either in a tree trunk or long gone. I had nothing to lose. I used the camera to sweep outward and zoom in on the trees. There were dozens of potential resting places for a bullet. I also couldn't know if the body itself had redirected its flight. It was a stab in the dark. Not even the detectives from Boone would be willing to take on the task. I was concerned about time so my search began.

There were more pines up here than the hardwoods that dominated the lower elevations. That made it hard to see the trunks except for close to the ground. I couldn't climb every tree I wanted to inspect. I also had to remain alert for intruders. It was difficult to direct my attentions to two separate tasks. Finding the bullet would require intense concentration. I'd need to focus, but dropping my guard could be deadly. It didn't take long before I considered it an impossible task. I broke off my search and returned to the opposite side of the pot plants. I looked and listened downward. I walked back the way I'd come for a few hundred yards before stopping.

Could I do it again? Did I really have that ability? I calmed myself and slowed my heart rate. I breathed deeply of the clean mountain air. I smelled the pines and the dirt. I listened to the slight rustling of the trees. It came to me again. Each sense expanded exponentially. I became ultra-aware of what the mountain had to say. I directed my attention even further downward and held it. I had no sense of time. I kept it up, but it may have only been minutes. No one was coming up the mountain from the camp. I was alone.

I hustled back to the trees that may have caught a bullet. I studiously examined each one. I looked for nicks in branches that might give me a clue. I pulled out the camera again and zoomed in on areas I couldn't reach. I found nothing. It was hopeless. I crept about in my deerskin shoes all afternoon. I was getting tired and I needed to figure out my sleeping arrangements before it got dark.

I went back towards the hunting shack and listened again until I was satisfied that no one was present or coming up the path. I didn't expect they would at this hour, but my survival depended upon staying one step ahead. I wished I knew where Pop's hideaway was. He'd revealed plenty about himself to me, but I guess the location of his home was something he wanted to remain a secret. Maybe after this was over I could hunt it down.

I walked ever-widening circles around the weed plants, looking for a decent spot to lie down. I didn't want to build anything yet. It might be spotted later and screw up the scene. I might leave clues implicating myself. I just wanted some cover and concealment. I didn't want to get eaten by a bear. I had to claw through those mountain mangrove rhododendrons until I found a hollow spot that would allow me to stretch out. I drank deeply and devoured some jerky before dark. It promised to be a long night. I thought about Brody down there in our cozy cabin. I knew she'd fret about me. I was so lucky to have her in my life. I'd promised her many things. Sleeping in the weeds on a mountain wasn't one of them. I'd make a strong effort to make it up to her, but for the night, I remained focused on my mission.

Hearing, seeing, and smelling at elevated levels made sleep difficult. I was there on the ground, hidden by weeds and trees, but haunted by what my senses perceived. What most people would consider silence was to me a cacophony of noise. I tried to count the different odors that reached my nose. I gave up at three dozen. At least darkness dimmed my vision. Finally, fatigue overtook me and I was able to block out the noise. In spite of my uncomfortable accommodations, I slept deeply.

Deep sleep brings on dreams. I had a history of profound dreams at times like this. After my wife's death, I saw her in my sleep. I could never reach her. My helplessness haunted me for a long time. I dreamt about a man I had beaten to death for a long time too. I always saw myself from above, flailing away at my opponent even after he stopped moving. It took years to shake my regret. On my last mission, I joined a team of experienced operators to rig the floodgates on Lake Okeechobee in order to flood the sugar cane fields. Just before we pulled it off, I had a dream where the small towns below the lake flooded badly. Thousands of people were drowning because of what I'd done. Then I was there in my boat, picking up victims. There were too many of them and the boat was swamped. That dream forced me to make changes to our plan of attack, in order to ensure the safety of those people.

I don't take vivid dreams lightly.

Eight

That night on the mountain I dreamt of staring down the barrel of a rifle. I couldn't see the face of the man aiming at me. A wisp of smoke left the weapon and the bullet raced towards me. Everything went black. I was lost in the darkness. I had no sense of myself. It was nothingness.

I was awake but it was still black. Low clouds obscured the moon. No light penetrated my den where I was bedded down. I was spooked by how the darkness in the dream morphed into real darkness. I lay still and composed myself. I had other senses to rely on. At first, I heard nothing, but gradually the sound of the creek became clear. I sniffed the air for the scent of any predators. I was okay. Nothing had found my hiding place. I sat up and poked my head out of the canopy. There was a faint ambient light after all. I focused on a tree until I gained my night vision.

I drank some water and nibbled on a piece of jerky, feeling more comfortable with my surroundings. It was just a dream. In the real world, I owned this mountain. I was the darkness and the light. I would decide who could trespass. It would not be some yokel deer hunter who'd kill a man for fifty pot plants.

I came out of the brush to stretch and relieve myself. I decided that each time I had to piss I'd pick a different tree. I'd mark my territory around the crime scene. I spent some time fiddling with the camera and checking my weapon. I ate a power bar. At the first hint of light, I set up in a good spot to surveil the plants. I was meticulous with my concealment, but I needed a good line of sight for the camera too. I went through the motions of picture taking to get a good feel for the light and the backdrop. That would change throughout the day, but if he came soon, I was ready for him.

I went over to the west side and went down a few hundred feet. I saw no one coming up. I heard nothing out of the ordinary. I'd just have to wait. I spent a few minutes reimagining the shot, trying to guess which trees to investigate for a bullet. It seemed hopeless. I poked around gently for a few hours. The plants needed water badly. The leather buckets were still where Pop had hidden them. Just after mid-morning, I took up my concealed position again.

It took two more hours of patiently waiting, but I heard a man climbing the other side of the hill. He was being cautious, but my superior hearing picked up on his errant footsteps. I could differentiate the slight noise he made from the natural sounds of the forest. I didn't smell him until he crested the hill. He smelled of soap and freshly laundered clothing. He was wearing camo hunting clothes, but no orange vest. He had a rifle slung over his shoulder. He was carrying a five-gallon bucket. For a moment he almost disappeared. He'd stopped and crouched down at the edge of the clearing, just inside the tree line. He remained still, making sure no one else was around. I knew he had to cross open territory before he reached the big rocks. I was ready with the camera. I got two full-body shots of the man while he was in the open. He knelt behind the boulder where I assumed he'd taken the shot. I focused on the space just above it. As soon as he poked his head out, I captured his face. He spent less than a minute there. He was confident that the coast was clear. I watched him stand and stroll casually towards the center of the pot patch. He unslung the rifle and propped it against a tree. I got a good close-up photo of it. He went to the creek and filled his bucket. He dumped the whole thing on the first plant he came to. Most of it ran off on the dry ground.

At this rate, he'd have to make fifty trips. Five gallons of water weighed roughly forty pounds. It would be a good workout for him. Meanwhile, he was tracking up the soil with his boots, leaving good evidence. Suddenly, he stopped mid-pour. He put the bucket down and stood up. He walked over to where Pop's body should have been. How could he have overlooked a missing dead man? Maybe he assumed a bear had dragged it off at first, but now he could see that there was no blood stain. The spot had been swept clean. He turned in a circle surveying the surrounding trees and rocks. I got several clear shots of his face as he stood there.

He obviously didn't know what to make of this development. He took his hat off and scratched his head. He kicked the dirt around, maybe looking for dried blood. Any decent deer hunter had to also be a tracker. Even a well-placed shot may not kill his quarry immediately. Big bucks have been known to cover quite a bit of ground before finally succumbing to their injury. He continued poking the dirt with his feet, moving around the site. He was baffled. He shrugged and went back to his bucket. Then he changed his mind and went for his rifle. He slung it back over his shoulder, making his travels with the bucket more difficult.

I had all the pictures that I needed. I concentrated on remaining invisible, while he worked. When he was at the creek with his back to me, I stowed the camera and undid the strap holding my pistol in its holster. I hoped I didn't need it, but the dream was a warning. The way I was dressed and hidden would let him know exactly what I was up to. There'd be no excuses made for what I was doing. It seemed like hours had passed before he was satisfied that the plants were all watered. He started to leave but stopped behind his big rock. He put down the bucket and the rifle. I watched him snap off a thin, low branch with plenty of leaves. He came back and started erasing his boot prints. I figured I could find some of his tracks on the way down the hill after he was gone, but the easy evidence was no more.

I got a real good look at him then. He was young, thirty at the most. His hair was close-cropped, almost a flattop and blond. He was fit but not like the type who works out daily. He was toned, not bulky. He was light on his feet and agile. If he thought someone might be watching, he had no discipline about it. He was careful when he first arrived, but he'd forgotten all that. He had a tough edge about him, though, like he'd seen his share of fights. I considered how I'd handle him if we came to blows. I'd seen my share of fights too, but my prime days were behind me. I usually depended on surprise to take out a bigger man. I certainly didn't stand toe to toe and let someone half my age take shots at me.

It wasn't that long ago when a true bear of a man had beat the snot out of me. I'd let my guard down and he'd been the one to surprise me. I had no chance. I wanted to avoid repeating that experience at all costs. I'd come up here to the mountains to rest and recuperate. This young hunter had spoiled my convalescence and disturbed my peace. I figured he ought to pay for that, but I hoped to give him the bill without violence. Eventually, Pop's death would have to be avenged. If the legal system couldn't accomplish that, I would.

Finally, he was satisfied with his efforts. He backed away from the plants, sweeping away his prints as he went. When he reached the rocks he took up his weapon and bucket and retreated down the mountain. I didn't move for another hour. I listened, frozen in my surveillance position. When I was certain he was long gone I came out of hiding. I followed his path until I found the first boot print. I took a picture and continued a little further. Every fifteen or twenty yards he left a print in the dry earth between rocks and logs. I snapped more pictures before turning around and heading back to my side of the mountain. I couldn't go down through the hunting camp. My enemy might be down there having a beer after his hard day's work.

I was happy with my progress. My pictures would tell the story. This man had diligently watered his crop. He'd snooped around in the dirt, where a body had once lain. He'd covered up his own footprints, surely a sign of guilt. It looked every bit as I hoped it would. If it got to court he'd be screwed, at least for the marijuana operation. The murder would be something else. I needed that bullet. There'd be no further looking for it that day. I had to get down the hill and home to Brody. I had to get my evidence to the Sheriff. I had to get a hot shower and a good meal.

I almost ran down the hill on the way home. I was starving for one thing, but I was excited for what I'd captured on camera. We would soon know who the killer was. Someone would identify the guy. No matter how inept or unconcerned local law enforcement was, they'd be forced to take action. I'd done what I could do to honor my friend.

Brody was waiting outside the back door with her arms crossed like she knew my arrival was imminent.

"I hope you haven't been standing here for the last two days," I said.

"I didn't figure you'd spend two nights up there," she said. "It's almost dark, time for you to come home."

"But the streetlights aren't on yet, mom," I said.

"Don't mom me," she replied. "Get in there and get cleaned up."

"I've got a lot to tell you," I said. "And lots of pictures of our suspect."

"So you're done up there?"

"Well, I'd like to find the bullet if I can," I said. "He watered the plants today. Likely won't be back soon."

"We go to the Sheriff first," she said. "If you're going back up there, I'm going with you. I can cover you while you search."

"Excellent idea," I said. "I knew I could count on you."

"You got us into this," she reminded me. "The least I can do is help get us out of it."

The Watauga County Sheriff's Department was on Hodges Gap Road, not far from Appalachian State University in Boone. It was adjacent to the Detention Center. When we arrived we discovered that the Sheriff himself wasn't available. We explained to the Deputy what we wanted to do. He set up Brody with a computer to download my photos. A few were blurry and not useful, but most were crisp enough to clearly identify the man on the mountain. The Deputy didn't know him. He assured us that he would make sure the Sheriff saw the pictures, as soon as he returned. There was nothing else we could do, so we left. We'd have to wait on the Sheriff.

I thought some more about the man. Our cabin and property were in Watauga County, but very close to the Avery County line.

Banner Elk was much closer than Boone but had no Sheriff's Department. The closest one was all the way down in Newland. We needed someone in law enforcement that knew our suspect. I decided to drive to the Banner Elk Police Department. We had to go through the whole story with the chief before he would even look at the pictures. He didn't want to step on the neighboring county's toes. He made it clear that his department would not participate in any investigation outside of its jurisdiction, which was within the town limits of Banner Elk only.

"If this guy is from Banner Elk or nearby, there's a chance no one in Boone will know who he is," I said. "If you know him, you can pass on his identity to the Sheriff."

"This alleged crime took place in Watauga County, right?" he said.

"And the guy may live in Watauga," I said. "But he may be known to the locals in Banner Elk. We're much closer to town down here than going to Boone."

"I'll take a look," he said. "But I can't discuss this further with you unless Sheriff Watts gives me the okay."

"You won't tell me who it is?"

"No sir, I will not," he said. "This is a police matter."

"But I'm the one solving the crime," I said. "A murder no less."

"I'll ask Watts to bring me up to speed," he said. "So far he hasn't asked for our help."

"I'd like for someone to let me know how the investigation progresses," I said. "But we don't have a phone. The Sheriff knows where we live."

"I'm sure he'll be in touch if he needs you," he said. "Have a fine afternoon."

"You've got pictures of a killer right there in front of you," I said. "Spend your afternoon figuring out who he is."

The cops around my new homestead sure had a casual attitude towards solving crime. I doubted there was much crime at all in Banner Elk. Boone was a college town. The cops there probably specialized in drunks and druggies. I didn't know much about what went on out in the counties. It was very rural, probably not much action for police officers. Still, I was spitting mad on the drive back to the cabin. I'd taken great pains and made a personal sacrifice to hand-deliver the identity of a killer to law enforcement. *We'll get back to you* wasn't good enough.

"What else can we do?" asked Brody.

"I need to talk to the Sheriff," I said. "In the meantime, we can look for that bullet."

"What if we run into our killer up there?"

"Plants have been watered," I said. "There's rain in the forecast. He won't risk coming back for a while."

"Then I guess we're going bullet hunting," she said. "You can teach me the ways of the mountain."

"I just learned a few things myself," I said. "Let's not pretend I'm Grizzly Adams."

"I think you look more like Jeremiah Johnson," she said. "You just need the beard."

I was half expecting the Sheriff to show up that afternoon. By the time we sat down to dinner, I knew he wasn't coming. We'd give him a few hours in the morning before we went up the hill. I was reasonably sure we'd be alone up there, so we didn't take all the precautions that I'd taken before. We had a relaxing evening and got a good night's sleep.

A police cruiser pulled down the drive just after nine the next morning. The Sheriff got out with a file folder in his hand. I invited him in and offered him coffee. We sat at the kitchen table and went over the pictures he'd printed out.

"I should say something about you going to the Banner Elk PD," he said. "But their chief knows our boy, so I'll let it pass."

"You're welcome," I said. "Who's our man?"

"Cody Banner," he said. "Umpteenth removed descendant of the original Banner family."

"What do you know about him?"

"The Chief passed along a little history," he said. "Troubled youth. Judge pushed him to go into the Army instead of jail. Seemed to turn him around for a while, but disciplinary problems eventually got him booted out of the service. He's had a few run-ins since coming home. Drunk and Disorderly, small-time possession, DUI, small stuff."

"Murder is not small stuff, Sheriff," I said.

"We're a long way from booking him for murder," he said.

"Fifty mature weed plants isn't small stuff either," I said. "It was big enough to kill Pop Sutton over."

"We don't know what went down," he said. "All we have is your conjecture."

"And my photos," I said. "What about the rifle?"

"It's a Remington Model 700," he said. "Wilderness rifle. Pretty common in the backcountry. Durable and the price is right."

"I don't know much about rifles," I said. "What round does it fire?"

"Another reason this gun is popular," he said. "It can handle a variety of loads. 270, 30.06, all the way up to the 300 Win Magnum."

"So if we found the bullet it would still be hard to narrow it down to that specific rifle?"

"Forensics lab could identify it if we had both the weapon and the bullet," he said. "We'd have to send them to Raleigh."

"So are you going to track this guy down and question him?" I asked. "At least about the dope?"

"I've taken the matter under consideration," he said.

I sifted through the pictures until I found the one I wanted.

"Here we have a known subject, watering what is clearly a pot plant," I said. "The man is armed with a high-powered rifle, but not hunting. A man was killed recently with just such a rifle. One plus one equals two, Sheriff."

"If it were only that simple," he said. "I'll be seeking advice from our legal minds before I make any kind of move on this. It's not cut and dried like you think it is."

"I'm certainly no legal mind," I said. "But if I get you that bullet, will you get a warrant for the rifle and see where it leads?"

"Even then, the defense would have a field day," he said. "You pull a random bullet out of a tree not far from Cody's hunting camp but not where the body was found. It won't tie him to the murder."

I seriously regretted moving the body and cleaning up the crime scene. I screwed the whole thing up. I was at a loss for what to do next. I looked to Brody for guidance. She'd been an investigator.

"I know it's circumstantial at best," she said to the Sheriff. "But you bring him in on dope charges and squeeze him. Pressure him until he's ready to plea. Avoid a trial."

"I should have paid more attention to the red flags your background check raised," he said. "One of you is former law enforcement, while the other was usually on the wrong side of the law. Quite the team you two have. On the other hand, maybe you're simply diverting suspicion from yourselves. You sneak into my county under the radar with shady pasts. A dead body turns up on your property and you shove your own personal investigation down my throat. Who's to say you're not framing this Banner fellow?"

"That's a ridiculous theory," said Brody.

"About as much evidence as you have," he said. "Short of sending an army to scour every blade of grass up there, I don't see how we can bring a case. We'll probably do something about the dope, but it's doubtful we'll clear up the murder."

"Pick him up and question him about Pop," Brody said. "Maybe he'll crack easy. Worth a try."

"I'll let you know if we get a break," he said. "I'll spare you the spiel about lack of staff and limited resources. That's just the way it is."

NINE

After he left we felt defeated. I'd convinced myself that the case against Pop's killer was a slam-dunk. Brody seemed to think they could still nail him by arresting him on trafficking charges and putting the screws to him over the murder. I felt that they lacked the enthusiasm for that strategy. Neither of us were lawyers, but we'd both had plenty of experience with the law, both good and bad. We were missing something. Why weren't they going after this guy with everything they had?

In the meantime, I'd try to find the bullet. I'd try to learn more about Cody Banner. He was practically my neighbor, after all. Maybe I could catch him at his hunting camp and shoot the shit, take stock of the man, buy him a beer. I'd have to keep an eye on him. If the cops didn't close in before harvest time, I couldn't just let him walk away with the crop. Certainly, catching him in the act would spur the cops to take action. One way or another, he was going down for something.

I got curious about the hunting seasons in the area. Fall was coming. Soon there'd be hunters in the woods on the other side of the mountain. I hadn't hunted since I was young. My father took me into the woods and taught me, but I lost interest in it in my adulthood. I'd been a good shot with a long gun, mainly a shotgun and a .22. As long as the target was still, I could take its eyes out at a hundred yards. In the Army, I qualified as a Sharpshooter with the M-16. I didn't miss out as far as three-hundred yards. My problem had been with fast-moving targets. Rabbits and ducks confounded me. I could hit a big, slowly dropping goose, but anything faster than that and I was terrible. It drove my father nuts. He took me out in a field and threw oil cans up in the air for me to practice on. I rarely hit one. Target shooting was another matter. Dad was a pro at the range, often hustling other shooters in contests of accuracy. I picked up that skill from my old man. I could split a matchstick with a .38 from twenty feet. Suddenly I wanted to buy a rifle. If it came down to a confrontation between me and Cody Banner, I needed to be on equal footing.

Brody and I drove down to Boone once again to visit High Country Tactical. The gun shop was on the main road from Banner Elk into Boone. At first, no one seemed interested in helping me, but when I asked for the Remington Model 700 they were all ears. I let them sell me a bunch of 30.06 ammo and an orange vest. I got a brochure for the Hunting Rules and Regulations of Watauga County. I stopped by the Sheriff's Department on the way home. I showed the Sheriff my receipt for purchase and the boxes of ammo, just so he'd know it was a new purchase.

"I've no interest in violating your Second Amendment rights," he said. "But this seems a curious purchase, considering the circumstances."

"There's a murderer loose on my mountain," I said. "Just looking for an even playing field.

Besides, I thought I'd do a little hunting this Fall."

"I haven't decided if you're a brave sumbitch or just stupid," he said. "I don't have to tell you to be careful up there. Wear your orange."

"Safety first," I said, giving him a wink.

I wanted him to know that I wasn't giving up on our little mystery. Maybe if he didn't want me to interfere, he'd get off his ass and do something. Meanwhile, I'd keep plugging away at my own investigation.

"What do you think about the bullet?" I asked Brody. "You think there are random bullets lodged in trees all over the mountain?"

"Not likely," she said. "But he has a point. If the body was left where it fell, it would be more obvious for a jury that the bullet we find is the one that killed him."

"What about DNA?" I asked.

"Finding Banner's DNA on this random bullet doesn't prove he killed Pop," she said. "Just that he once fired off a shot not far from his hunting camp."

"No," I said. "I meant Pop's DNA."

"It's theoretically possible," she said. "But extremely difficult. The FBI is probably the only agency that could come close."

"It just so happens that you have a friend in the FBI," I pointed out. "One who's taken a personal interest in our activities."

"This isn't an FBI matter," she said.

"Can't local law enforcement ask for their help in certain cases," I asked. "Like complicated forensics?"

"Other than serial killings, forensics is the main reason the locals call the FBI," she explained. "But it's not a common practice. They're called the Feds because they investigate federal crimes. This hardly qualifies."

"These particular locals can't even get striations off a bullet without sending it to Raleigh," I said. "They really don't have the resources needed to solve this."

"They have to be the ones to ask the Bureau for help," she said. "The FBI can't just come in and take over, despite what you may have seen on TV."

"I think your buddy could possibly persuade them that they needed help," I said. "Make a sincere offer of assistance."

"It's no good without that bullet," she said. "We're just playing a game of what-if until we find it."

"Then I guess we know what we need to do," I said. "You still up for climbing around our mountain?"

"I'm game."

In my head, I knew that finding the bullet was a fool's errand, but my heart drove me on anyway. For the time being, we were at a standstill. Searching for it would give me something to do. It would also get Brody up in the woods with me, which was something I wanted for us to share. In a short time, I'd put the Florida landscape behind me, trading it for the Blue Ridge Mountains. I didn't intend to look back.

We climbed the hill the very next day after I'd picked up a new pair of Merrell's from the Little Red School House. Brody stuck with her boots. She carried the Smith & Wesson and I carried the new rifle. We traveled light, with just water and a few snacks. We moved quickly for the first half of the hike until I stopped her and told her to sit down.

"Get your breath," I said. "Try to relax. Bring your heart rate down. Just be for a minute."

"Zen and the art of mountain climbing?"

"Something like that," I said. "Let's just sit still and chill out for a few minutes."

We sat quietly for five full minutes. I was hearing more than before, seeing and smelling more.

"Listen," I said. "Really listen."

"For what?"

"What do you hear?" I asked.

"The creek," she said. "Some birds."

"Okay, concentrate on those sounds," I instructed. "Listen beyond them. Try to hear the background noise."

"I hear the breeze on the leaves now," she said. "Didn't notice that before."

"Good," I said. "Now allow the sounds to be amplified. What else is there that you didn't hear at first?"

"Us," she said. "We make little sounds every time we move. My own breathing. Your breathing."

"I'm going to shut up now," I said. "Take a few more minutes. Take in all the noises."

We sat in silence, totally still, for another ten minutes. Brody gave me a look. She was starting to experience it. She nodded but held up a hand for me to remain still and quiet. I let her drift off into her own mountain zone for a while. I did nothing until she spoke.

"I'll admit I hear a lot more," she said. "But not like having a bionic ear or anything."

"What do you smell?"

"Earth," she said. "Soil, leaves, bark."

"Take a minute to explore the smells further," I said. "Go beyond the obvious."

Again I left her alone to do her own thing. She was receptive to the idea. She trusted me. She took another ten minutes or so to concentrate on smells.

"Okay, I smell myself," she said. "Soap and shampoo and my clean clothes. I can smell you too, but you're so close. Same thing. We're clean people in the wilderness."

"Any natural odors?"

"Pine," she said. "And I think the creek itself has a smell. Something crisp and clean."

"There's oak and poplar and birch too," I said. "Not as aromatic as pine, but still there."

"It's very subtle," she said. "I sensed more but didn't know what they were."

"You're off to a great start, grasshopper," I said. "Ready to move on?"

"Onward and upward."

"There's no one else up here," I said. "But stay alert like always. I'm going to move quickly so we have time to search when we get there."

"I'm following you," she said.

My legs had become more accustomed to all the climbing, but it was still hard work. Brody hadn't done nearly as much hiking as I had, so she tired quickly.

"My hamstrings are on fire," she said. "I need to stop for a minute."

"Take a break," I said. "Practice tuning in your senses."

"I need to catch my breath first," she said. "Is it this steep all the way up?"

"For the most part," I said. "You'll get better at it."

Brody pulled herself together and we moved on. We'd get plenty of rest at the top, and the trip down would be much easier. As we neared the pot patch, I signaled for her to slow down and listen. I didn't expect company, but we couldn't be too careful. We crouched together and surveyed the site. There was no trace of another human. I whispered for her to cover me while I went to the other side and checked down the hill. There were no signs of life there either. The search could begin.

I showed Brody where I thought the shot was fired from.
"Anyone coming will approach from here," I said, pointing down the western slope. "I'll be over there poking around in the trees."
"Got it," she said. "I'll set up here and listen for anything out of the ordinary."

For the third or fourth time, I attempted to triangulate the path of the bullet. I walked over the spot where the body had fallen and towards the bullet's likely resting place. I carefully inspected each potential tree. I even looked for nicks in the bark where the bullet may have glanced off. It was a slow and tedious process. I lowered my level of alertness to outside stimuli, trusting that Brody had my back. I needed to focus all of my concentration on the task at hand. My eyes scoured every square inch of tree trunk and lower branch over a fifty-yard square area. At least three hours passed with nothing found. I came up empty.

I walked over to Brody and she offered to trade places with me for a while. I gladly accepted. I propped myself behind the shooter's big rock and faced toward Cody Banner's hunting camp. I let Brody do her thing and paid attention to the sights and sounds of the hillside. I hefted our new rifle and looked down its sights, aiming at a random tree. If it came down to it, could I shoot a man with it? I'd fired a weapon during violent situations in my past, but it was always in order to save my life. An assassin was drawing a gun and I had no time to think it over. I simply reacted. A drug runner was ripping apart my boat with an automatic weapon. I blasted in his direction with my shotgun, barely aiming. Looking down the barrel of this rifle was another feeling altogether. You could take a man out at several hundred yards with a weapon like this. He'd never know who shot him. It took a cold-blooded killer to do something like that. I wasn't sure I had it in me.

I heard Brody call for me. I turned and she waved for me to come over. She then pointed up, higher in the trees. I noticed that she was slightly downhill from me as I walked towards her. I recalculated the possible path of the bullet. It may have hit higher than I'd been searching. Brody had already figured that out.

"If it hit one of these trees," she said. "It's got to be up there. Higher than we can see very well."

"Any ideas?"

"A ladder, I guess," she said. "Or one of those climbing tree stand things the hunters use."

"I've never used one," I said. "Don't know if it would mark up the trees, or even how to work it."

"So we need a nice light ladder," she said. "Ten feet or more."

"That's going to be a bitch to carry all this way," I said.

"I don't see what other option we have."

"We could build one up here," I said. "Bring an ax or saw, some nails and a hammer."

"Spoken like a real mountain man," she said. "You really are adapting to this life, aren't you?"

"I like it," I said. "It feels good to be close to the land. You can never own the water. It just allows you passage. This mountain feels like home."

"Welcome home, Breeze."

We had a bite to eat and drank some water before departing. I picked a new tree to continue my marking of the territory. The hike back down was ten times easier than the climb up. It took half the time. It was good to have our cabin as a refuge. We both felt safe there, regardless of what might happen outside our doors. I'd split and stacked most of the wood on the porch. We'd purchased a generator in case the power went out over the winter months. We bought some warm clothes. We were actually looking forward to the first snowfall.

We drove into Banner Elk the next day to visit Lowes. I bought a sharp hand saw, stout nails, a lightweight hammer, and a roll of thick twine. I'd never built a ladder before, but how hard could it be? We spent the rest of the day catching up on chores. There was no word from the Sheriff's Department or the Banner Elk PD.

We climbed back up the mountain on fresh legs. Brody made it with less difficulty and fewer rest periods. We went through our safety protocol before starting to build a ladder. The coast was clear. I hunted around for straight saplings or long branches to fashion the outside rails. The new saw cut nicely. I cut another branch into smaller sections to form the rungs. Brody put a nail in each juncture and I wrapped them up with the twine. It wasn't pretty, but it would do the job.

Brody was much lighter than I, so she got the ladder climbing duties. I stayed on the ground with the rifle strapped over my shoulder. After deeming a tree bullet-free, we'd move on to the next. We worked all afternoon in vain. We were both frustrated.

"It must have missed all these trees and gone out over the ridge," she said. "No finding it down there."

"We should have bought a metal detector," I said. "We could sweep all around the trunk and branches until it beeps. Wouldn't even have to see it first."

"You might have thought about that yesterday," she said. "But it's a good idea."

"Getting a little slower in my old age," I said.

"Let's call it a day, grandpa," she said. "Come back with a metal detector."

I dragged our homemade ladder deep into the brush, away from the pot plants. The hike back downhill was a breeze.

Ten

We had to drive to Boone to find a metal detector. I found a good one that wasn't too heavy. We played around with it in the yard to dial in the sensitivity. Afterward we set up an improvised target out behind the cabin. We each fired a few rounds with the rifle. The early results were not promising. Brody said we needed sandbags to rest the weapon on. We were a long way from sand, so we used a stump from the woodpile instead. We both shot better, but still not stellar. I watched as Brody fiddled with the sights and tried again. She repeated the process until she could hit the center of the target multiple times in succession.

I took my turn behind the stump. I relaxed my arms and slowed my breathing. I lined up the sights, let out one last breath slowly, and pulled the trigger. The bullet hit the target just a fraction of an inch from Brody's best shot. I pulled off a second shot that was equally accurate. We were satisfied that our weapon was ready and that we could wield it effectively. Brody loaded a backpack with supplies before we called it a day.

We sat on the porch with a cold beer and watched the creek roll by. A doe came down for her daily dose of apples. Squirrels chased each other around a birch tree. Hummingbirds buzzed the flowers and Brody's feeder.

"I really love this place, Breeze," Brody said. "I'm so grateful to live here."

"Sure is peaceful," I said. "Other than that whole killer on the loose thing."

"We're doing what we can," she said. "Why do you suppose the cops are sitting on their hands?"

"I'm not sure," I admitted. "Incompetence, lack of incentive. Maybe the guy is connected. His name is Banner. The sheriff said he was a descendant of the original Banner family."

"But we're talking about murder," she said. "They can't cover it up like a DUI."

"It's a murder that would be damn hard for them to solve," I said. "They don't want to put in the kind of effort that we've been putting in. It's hard work."

"So what about the weed?"

"I really thought they'd do something about that," I said. "But attitudes are changing about dope. It's barely a crime anymore. I got caught with two pounds and managed to get probation."

"Thanks to a crooked lawyer."

"And money," I told her. "The lawyer's services didn't come cheap. I'm sure I indirectly contributed to the bribe as well."

"You've never really talked about money," she said. "You just seemed to always have it since we met."

"Long story," I said. "I'll try to condense it for you. I was broke. Like going hungry broke. I barely survived at all until I got a settlement from my wife's untimely death. I managed to lose the entire fortune and was broke again. I could recover what I'd lost, but I needed cash to go after it. I started running drugs for a kingpin in the Keys. First, it was only bales of weed that I picked up from shrimpers near the

Tortugas. Eventually, it became a ton of cocaine picked up in Columbia."

"Jesus, Breeze," she said. "I had no idea."

"It ain't pretty," I said. "But I was eventually able to recover the money I'd lost. I had to go to the Dominican to get it though. Bribing judges and paying lawyers ate most of it up anyway."

"You went broke again?"

"Pretty much," I told her. "Then I started working for Captain Fred. It became quite lucrative. Money hasn't been a problem since."

"But you can't work for him from here," she said. "Not that I want you to."

"We're sitting on a million dollars," I said. "The house is paid for. Our bills are few. If we don't live to be one-hundred we should be fine."

"Now that's a retirement plan," she said. "Die before the money runs out."

"I've never been big on planning."

"I've noticed, trust me," she said. "But if the cops don't make a move on this Banner guy, we'll need to have a plan. You can't just wing it like you usually do. He's already killed at least once."

"For now, I'm hoping the bullet will spur someone to action," I said. "If we don't find it we'll have to seriously regroup."

"It feels like an impossible long shot," she said. "If it's not in a tree, we can't sweep the whole valley for it."

"I wish I could tell you that I had a gut feeling we were going to find it," I said. "I keep trying to summon that feeling, but it hasn't come. Let's give it another shot with the metal detector. If we don't find it tomorrow, we'll give up looking."

We got a very early start. The sun wasn't up yet, but the lower part of the climb was the easiest part to manage in the dark. I carried both the backpack and the detector to allow Brody an easier passage. Each got a bit heavier as we climbed, slowing me down. I decided to stop short of our destination to rest and up our awareness level.

"I can take one of those now," said Brody.

"I got it," I said. "I need you to take the lead on listening and looking while I play pack mule. You good with that?"

"Give me a minute to get in the mood," she said.

"That's not what you said last night," I joked.

"Let me settle down," she said. "Stay quiet."

We rested and calmed things down. I tuned in to the sounds of the woods. We sat there together in silence and became one with the mountain. After a few minutes, Brody nodded. She was ready. She took the lead and I followed with my burdens. I pulled her up short of the weed farm. I wasn't sure if she knew we were about to arrive. We communicated silently. I put down my load and she covered me while I checked the opposite slope. There was no sign that anyone had been there. There was no sign that anyone was approaching. We were clear to renew our search.

I pulled the makeshift ladder out of the bushes and dragged it back to the search area. Before we started sweeping the trees, we went back to the rock where I was sure the shooter had fired from. I asked Brody to do her own triangulation. That first day I was positive I'd found the right spot, but now I was wavering.

I'd been in the zone that day. My perception of events was hypersensitive. I'd been certain of what I perceived. Brody signaled me to be still and I watched as she tuned into a Zen-like state. She didn't just look over the scene, she felt its vibrations. She stepped one way, then another, holding her arms out.

"He was here," she said, pointing at the big rock. "But he may have fired from over here."

She led me to another rock.

"This one is a better shooting platform," she said. "He could have crawled unseen to get a better vantage point. That changes our search pattern significantly."

She held her arm out towards the trees and shifted it back and forth. I stood behind her to see what she saw. We were to the right of the first rock. The angle placed the bullet to the left of our original search area. There were only a few trees blocking the bullet's path from its inevitable descent into the valley below.

"Let's get started," I said. "Shouldn't take long."

I dragged the ladder to our new search area. We started with the tree closest to what we'd already searched. I propped up the ladder, Brody went up, and I handed her the metal detector. It was an awkward process but she swept the tree up and down and all around. There was no beep. She came down and we moved the ladder. We got a beep on the third tree. Neither of us could see anything. She continued to sweep until she narrowed the beep down to a specific spot.

"It's under this elbow here," she said. "What now?"

"Let's move the ladder for a better look," I said.

After repositioning the ladder, I went up for a closer inspection. I found a hole on the underside of a branch right where it joined the main trunk. It was just a hole. I couldn't prove it was a bullet without doing some digging. I didn't think we ought to tamper with the evidence, but could we get someone up here to dig it out? If it was DNA we were after, we definitely shouldn't touch it.

"What do you think?" I asked. "Mark the spot and try to get the cops up here?"

"The FBI would be better," she said. "But I don't see how we can enlist them."

"We leave it where it's at," I said. "Try to get the law up here. I've got some other ideas in the meantime."

"Like what?"

"I think it's time to meet this Banner fellow," I said. "At least find out some more about him."

"We'll go to the Sheriff first," she said. "You can do your sleuthing afterward."

I jammed a stick in the ground on the backside of the tree that contained our bullet. It would be easy to find. I struggled with the stupid ladder again until it was hidden away. It had been a long day, but we thought we'd found what we were looking for. I let Brody carry the metal detector on the way back home. Our discovery was a bit anti-climactic. Without the actual bullet, our work wasn't done, but we needed to preserve the evidence if we hoped to use it to make a case against Banner.

We went to visit the Sheriff first thing in the morning. He acted annoyed to see us.

"It would be easier if you just called," he said.

"We missed your smiling face," I said. "But we found the bullet."

"I told you it wouldn't make any difference," he said. "You're wasting both our time."

"Brody says that the FBI can extract DNA from a bullet," I told him. "Not just Banner's, but Pop's."

"It's shaky science from what I understand," he countered. "Especially if the DNA is compromised by being lodged in a tree for a week."

"Let the FBI examine it," said Brody. "If there's an iota of Pop's DNA we'll know it was the bullet that killed him. Then all you have to do is connect that bullet to Banner."

"You've watched too much CSI," he said. "I've got to have an ironclad reason to call in the Feds. Two newcomers traipsing around the woods isn't enough."

His comments didn't sit well with Brody. I could see it in her eyes. I saw her jaw muscles flexing.

"I know the pertinent statutes well," she began. "I'm sure I could construe at least one of them to peak the Bureau's interest here. Hiding or ignoring evidence that may clearly solve a murder is basically obstruction of justice, for starters. Not having the wherewithal to analyze that evidence if you did have it, is another. As you are aware, I still have some personal contact with the FBI."

"It was my impression that your relationship was not a pleasant one," he said. "And Mr. Breeze here has been on their wanted list more than once. You've got no standing to tell me how to run my department. Neither does the FBI."

"We're trying to help you," I said. "We brought you pictures of the guy. We got the Banner Elk PD to identify him. We're pretty sure we've located the bullet. What's it going to take to get you to act?"

"You're not going to get me or my men to crawl around in the bush on some godforsaken mountain looking for a stray bullet from any number of hunters," he said. "It's a fool's errand."

"What about the weed?" asked Brody.

"Nobody cares about some weed plants in the wilderness," he said. "Not worth our time."

"You leave us no choice then," said Brody. "We'll call the FBI ourselves."

"You won't get the time of day," he said. "Now get out of my office."

We'd accomplished nothing. I wasn't sure what to do next. We both fumed over the situation on the ride home. I was used to the cops being very interested in every little move I made. It was my experience that law enforcement was more than happy to participate in the actual enforcement of any law, no matter how small. The little guy always got screwed that way. Oh, you've got a little weed on you? Off to jail. Couldn't afford the bail money? Enjoy your stay in the clink. What we'd encountered here just didn't make sense. A rural Sheriff should be all over a murder case. Other than the low social status of the deceased, I couldn't figure out why he wasn't.

Who was Cody Banner? Why did he have immunity? There had to be some reason that this case wasn't being pursued. I needed to learn more about him. I needed more information. I told Brody to open a line of communication with her ex-lover, Bowdich. I'd figure out a way to get a line on Banner.

"We've still got that encrypted SAT phone," she said. "Time to dust it off."

"Good idea," I said. "I'd forgotten all about it."

After charging the thing up, Brody started trying to reach Bowdich. He didn't answer. She texted him to let him know that the strange number was her. He immediately called back. I went outside and let them talk. I took the rifle with me. I crouched behind the stump and sighted in the target we'd left on the hill behind the cabin. My first shot was dead center. The noise rang in my ears for a few seconds, triggering something. I sat and listened to the mountain. I smelled the gunpowder wafting around my face. I imagined that I could sense a man high up on the mountain, checking on the pot plants. I re-established my aim on the target. My second shot was as perfect as the first. *I'm coming for you, Banner.*

Eleven

Brody came outside without the phone. She looked annoyed that I'd fired the rifle while she was talking. Maybe it was a subconscious protest against her speaking with an ex-lover. I didn't feel threatened by him, though. I knew what Brody and I had together. Hell, she'd talked intimately with Holly, one of my exes.

"Drug-related murders are often prosecuted under federal laws," she said. "Our only other option is if our guy committed or commits another murder in a different state."

"Sure seems drug related to me," I said. "Banner killed Pop over a drug crop."

"No witness, no bullet, no weapon," she said. "David almost sounded as bad as the Sheriff."

"They don't know that Pop first owned the weed," I said. "But I do. Now we have the guy tending to the crop."

"As far as D.C. is concerned, it's just some yokel growing weed out in the boonies," she said. "They can't see how this is a drug murder."

"Then I need to talk to Bowdich," I said. "Start at the beginning and tell him the whole truth."

"Hearsay," she said. "You didn't witness the killing."

"If nobody cares about the weed, then no one should care that I was up there and aware of it," I said. "I should be free to tell my story."

"Seems like no one cares about the killing either," she said. "We're at a dead-end here, Breeze."

I had been too close to it. To me, it was obvious what happened up there. I cared about bringing Banner to justice. It was less obvious to everyone else, and they simply didn't care like I did. I could not, however, simply go shoot Banner myself. I couldn't let myself take killing so lightly. It would change me forever. If Banner had to walk in order for me to preserve my sanity, so be it, but I would try everything I could think of to make sure he didn't get away with it.

I just didn't know how yet.

I took a few days to think about my next course of action. I split wood with vigor, releasing some of my frustrations. We hiked to a few waterfalls that were nearby. We ate well and slept well. We made love like it mattered. We enjoyed our new cabin life, but unfinished business irked us both. After a week, I couldn't take it anymore. I needed to do something.

Downtown Banner Elk had no serious drinking establishments. It had fine restaurants. Some even had bars. I needed a place where a man stopped for a few beers on his way home from work. I drove around looking for a bar. I settled on the Flat Top Brewing Company just outside of town. I took a seat and was handed a beer menu. It wasn't a blue collar kind of place. It was a craft brewery. I ordered a Wunderbier and took a look around. It was a younger crowd, wearing nicer clothes. There wasn't a pair of work boots in the place. I wouldn't find Banner here, or even someone who might know him.

"Cody Banner ever stop in here?" I asked the bartender.

"Couldn't tell you," he said. "If he did he didn't tell me his name."

"You don't know a Cody Banner?"

"Can't say that I do."

I left him a buck tip for the eight dollar beer and left. I drove back to Pigeon Roost Road and stopped at the tracks leading uphill to the hunting camp. I parked off the edge of the road and walked towards the cabin. I didn't sneak up there. I walked normally and made some noise as I went. I didn't need a drunk hunter taking a shot at me. I found the cabin deserted. I kicked around the yard for a minute like I expected someone to show. No one did. I retreated back down the hill and went home to Brody.

"How'd it go?" she asked.

"Zilch, nada, nope," I answered. "I need to find a real bar where a man like him would stop. A place where folks know him. I just don't see it downtown."

"We don't know much about the town," she said. "Let's take a day and get a closer look. It'll be fun."

The next day we parked off the street in what served as the town's free parking area. We walked a few blocks and poked our head inside each restaurant. Barra's Sports Bar had a bunch of TV's hanging on the wall and was worth a try. None of the other spots looked to be a likely hangout for Banner. We drove beyond the town limits and found Nick's Pub. It was worth looking into as well. We made our way back through town and turned left on 194 instead of going back home. We found ourselves in Elk Park. There was a small country kitchen but no bar. Next, we hit Roan Mountain, first stop across the Tennessee line.

We found a place called The Station and went inside. It looked like a good old-fashioned bar but sold a strange combination of crafty IPA's and hot dogs. It was busy. The clientele looked like hikers mostly. We listened to hiker talk and got a feel for the place. I didn't picture Banner hanging out here but asked the bartender anyway.

"Do you know a guy named Cody Banner?"

"He's been in a few times," he said. "Lives nearby."

"No kidding," I said. "I believe he has a hunting property near my place."

"He's a big hunter," he said. "Always out in the woods come season."

"You say he lives around here?"

"Head west and make the first left," he instructed. "Single-wide on the right with a rusty pickup in the drive. That's him."

"Thanks, man."

I slid him a ten spot and got up to leave. Brody and I didn't talk until we got in the car.

"He lives in Tennessee," I said. "He crossed state lines to commit a murder."

"If he killed someone in Tennessee we've got something," she said.

"Shall we pay him a visit then?"

"I think we should be armed when we do that," she said. "Just saying."

"You're probably right," I said. "Who knows how he'll react."

"We don't have carry permits here," she pointed out.

"I don't suppose he'll call the cops on us."

We decided to go on home and come back better prepared. Brody went over our handguns that night, checking and cleaning even though they hadn't been fired. I wondered why Banner had a hunting camp in North Carolina when he lived in some great looking wilderness area in Tennessee. A few minutes with a map told me why. His mountain was one gigantic state park. It was obviously popular with hikers and therefore hunting was off-limits.

If I didn't catch him at his trailer, I'd certainly find him at the hunting camp once the season opened, if not before. He'd be out scouting and building tree stands in advance, probably baiting as well. As a neighboring property owner, it would be natural for me to introduce myself. I'd be concerned about him hunting on my property and so forth. I'd get a feel for the man, look him in the eye.

We drove back to Roan Mountain, made the first left past The Station and looked for a single-wide on the right. The bartender had specifically said rusty pickup. He didn't say Ford, Chevy, or Dodge. Everybody in eastern

Tennessee drove a pickup, as opposed to Banner Elk where it seemed everyone drove a Subaru. We saw no rusty pickup at any of the half-dozen trailers along that road.

On the way back we stopped again down below the hunting cabin. I took Brody up what passed for a driveway and showed her the place. I explained its proximity to the weed farm higher up the hill. It still looked as if no one had been there for a while.

"Talk about roughing it," she said. "What a dump."

"They probably spend most of their time in the woods," I said. "Just sleep here, have a few beers before the next day's hunt."

"I can picture three or four good old boys sitting around a fire out here," she said. "Chewing tobacco and lying about their sexual conquests."

"Murica!" I said. "Guns and alcohol and pickup trucks."

Back at the cabin I sat on the porch and thought things through, trying to regroup. In the past, I'd always been quick-witted in unusual situations. I never had a plan, I just winged it and hoped for the best. I was fast on my feet and ready to improvise no matter what was thrown my way. I was out of touch with living dangerously, and out of practice. I was also a step slower, and more averse to pain. When life didn't really matter much, I'd dive right in and take my lumps. Now my life with Brody was great. I didn't want to put myself in a position to cause myself harm or screw up what we had together. I certainly wanted to make sure that she remained free from harm.

I needed to take a step back and rearrange my thoughts on this one. I'd crashed and burned my way into someplace that no one thought I belonged. I'd pushed the Sheriff until he dismissed me completely. I didn't make friends with Bowdich from the FBI and now we could use his help. I tried to come at the problem from a different angle. I wasn't having much luck running into Banner on my own. Who knew him? Who knew how I could find him without raising unnecessary suspicion? I thought about the police chief down in Banner Elk. He'd passed on some preliminary information to the Sheriff concerning Banner. His department was aware of Banner's existence, and my claim that he was a killer. It wasn't up to them to solve the crime, but maybe they had more information that I could use. I decided to go to town the next day to talk to the chief.

When we first moved to the mountains I didn't like going to town. We were up at four-thousand feet and well-secluded. I didn't have to deal with people. It was peaceful and safe. Now it seemed driving down the mountain was an everyday occurrence. I'd much rather be hiking up in the woods.

The chief didn't throw us out. He seemed curious about our continued involvement. He likely had seen our background checks as well. His curiosity got the best of him and he agreed to sit down with us for a few minutes.

"I'm simply trying to put together some more information on Cody Banner," I told him. "I'm not asking you to interfere in someone else's investigation."

"I hear there is no investigation," he said. "I can't change that for you. I shouldn't even be talking to you, but I think you're trying to do the right thing. I've got an officer here who grew up with Banner. They went to high school together. I'll ask him if he wants to speak with you, but it can't be on the department's time or dime."

"I understand," I said. "That would be great. I appreciate it."

"You didn't get this information from me," he said. "Any conversations will have to take place away from this property or any of my patrol cars."

"Strictly unofficial," I said. "Just two guys having a chat. Not police business."

"Exactly," he said. "If he agrees, I'll send him up to your place after his shift."

"We'll go home and wait," I said. "Thanks, Chief."

Officer Holloway pulled down the drive in a Ford pickup just after dinner. He was in civilian clothes. He had a flat-top haircut under his Appalachian State ball cap. He was fit and strong looking but moved with an easy grace. He looked very much like a cop. We shook hands and Brody brought all of us a beer. He accepted with a southern *thank you, ma'am.*

"Thanks for agreeing to talk with us," I said. "I know it may seem a strange request."

"I probably know Cody as well as anyone," he said. "At least I used to, but part of why I'm here is really an off-the-books message from the chief."

"He doesn't want me poking around in local business?" I asked.

"It's not that really," he said. "Just wants you to know what you're getting mixed up in."

"My guess is that Banner is connected somehow," I said. "So nobody wants to go after him."

"Bingo," he said. "Connected and then some, but his connections are growing tenuous. Something like this might break through it all."

"Who is protecting him?" I asked.

"It's a double whammy," he explained. "His father is a big man around here. Developer, investor, civic associations. He's responsible for most everything that's been built around here over the past couple decades. He's got a stake in the resorts, golf courses, and the airport."

"Yet his son lives in a dumpy trailer and drives a rusty truck," I said.

"His father may be rich," he said. "But he came by it honestly. Started out building one house at a time down in the valley. He's earned everything he's ever gotten. That's what he wanted for Cody. He won't support him financially."

"But he'll make the law stand down when his boy gets into trouble."

"He doesn't even have to make them do anything," he said. "It's just because of who he is. Everyone wants to stay in his good graces. His grandfather is a different story, though."

"The double whammy," I said.

"Right. Granddad is a career politician," he said. "He's been the state senator for these parts for like a hundred years. These counties up here in this part of the state are his kingdom."

"And he'll strong arm anyone messing with his grandson," I said.

"He'd outright ruin them," he said. "The reason he never ran for federal office is all the corruption that he gets away with here. He'd rather be a big fish in a little pond. He pulls most of the strings from here to Charlotte."

"You said Banner's relationship with his father and grandfather were strained?"

"They always backed him whatever dumb thing he did," he said. "When we were teenagers he was constantly in trouble. Always had a tendency towards violence and destruction. He got in deep eventually. The judge was persuaded to advise him to enlist rather than go to jail. His father delivered him to a recruiter's office the next day. Thought it would do him good."

"But he got kicked out of the army."

"That's where it started to go downhill between him and his dad," he said. "It embarrassed him in the community. Granddad was unfazed. He's a different breed from a different time. Kind of a high country mafia figure."

"High country mafia?" I asked. "Can't say that I've ever heard that phrase."

"It's one of my own," he said. "But you know what I mean. Boss Hogg. Buford Pusser."

"The ultimate law is the grandfather."

"Correct," he said. "Cody does enough kissing the ring to make the old man happy. Takes him venison and shine. Helps around the yard."

"Is all of this intended to discourage me?"

"Vigilante justice is a tough business for an outsider," he said. "No one will support you, no matter how right you are."

"So we all just live with a killer in our midst?"

"We can't do anything," he said. "Maybe you can. It might wake granddaddy up. It would likely relieve his father. Cody is a menace. He's also smart and tough. I recommend you think long and hard before proceeding."

"Will the law come after me if I ruffle some feathers?" I asked.

"The Chief won't," he said. "That's part of why I'm here. Can't say the same for that Sheriff, or even the state boys."

"State troopers?"

"All conscripted by the Senator," he warned. "Watch your back."

"Christ," I said. "Thanks for the warning, I guess. Doesn't sound too promising."

"Just keeping it real for you," he said. "You're not in Florida anymore."

I got myself a shot of Tennessee whiskey and another beer after he left. I paced the cabin, absorbing all the new information that told me the obstacles were insurmountable. I was way out of my league with this one. I'd once delved into the legal and political system in Florida, but this was beyond my resources. I didn't have my old benefactor, Captain Fred, to rely on. I didn't know any of the players, not even Banner. If I'd have caught him on video murdering Pop it probably still wouldn't matter.

"What do you think, Brody?"

"I think you bit off more than you can chew," she said. "I also think that won't stop you from blundering on."

"I do not blunder," I said. "At least not anymore."

"What can we do?" she asked. "Our hands are tied."

"There are roadblocks, I'll give you that," I said. "We go around. Locks are made to be broken and all that. There's got to be a way."

"Let me know when you find it," she said. "I support you, but I don't see what else we can do."

"Me neither," I admitted. "Not yet, but I'll think of something."

A little devil appeared on my left shoulder and told me I should just execute Pop's killer.
"You're good with that rifle," he said. "He won't know what hit him and it will all be over with.
A little angel appeared on my right shoulder.
"Thou shall not kill," she said. "You are not a killer."

Except that I had been a killer. I killed a man with my bare hands. It was a very intense and personal thing. I'd lost my humanity long enough to take another man's life. I'd become an animal. When I regained my sanity the realization of what I'd done crushed my soul. I hadn't sought out the conflict. I was challenged by a younger man wanting to dethrone me as leader of the pack. I defended myself but didn't stop at that. I made him pay for his transgression. I made him pay with his life. What I'd done disturbed me so badly I dedicated my life to helping others. I tried to do enough good to even the scales of karmic justice. Brody had helped me tremendously in that quest. Together we'd spread goodwill and charity from Florida to Puerto Rico to the Virgin Islands. Every good thing that happened to me I turned into a way to pay it forward. I learned to be unselfish and to appreciate truly helping others. I learned to be kind.

Killing Banner now would erase my good deeds and doom me to a life in hell or worse. I needed a way to penetrate his force field of political protection, but I couldn't take on the Watauga County Sheriff, the State Police, and a senator. I was a simple boat bum, now floundering in the mountains. If I tried to forget it ever happened, I knew that it would ruin our new life here. I had to find a way through this so that we could then live happily ever after. But how?

I thought back to my early days in Florida. My pretty lawyer lady had gotten herself involved in corruption. She developed a team of judges and politicians that were easily bribed in an effort to advance her career. When things went sour for her, she threatened to expose me as someone who benefited from her bribery, which was true. I couldn't go to prison, so I turned on her. What followed was ugly and sordid. At the same time, I'd set up a fake PAC to influence an upcoming election. Three friends and a laptop convinced south Florida that I was a powerful political player, with lots of shadow money behind me. Of course, the money didn't exist, but our PAC raised a ton of cash in support of the Clean Water Movement. I used an alterego to singlehandedly convince one of the good guys to run for office in support of our platform. Looking back, it was pretty heady stuff. Could I do something like that again?

I knew that the FBI investigated the types of political corruption hinted at by Holloway, but if various law enforcement agencies were cowed by Banner's grandfather, I certainly couldn't make an impact. I didn't even know if the old man was a Republican or a Democrat. I had no idea exactly what kinds of crimes he may have committed. In order to do some research, we'd need a computer and a service provider. We'd moved here with the intent to leave the digital world behind. I'd get Brody to see if the Avery County Library could give us computer access.

Then there was Cody Banner himself. If I got to know him, could I record him incriminating himself in Pop's murder? If so, would that be enough? Where did the man work? Where did he hang out beside the hunting cabin? What kind of social setting could I create in order to befriend him?

I continued working through the multi-layered challenge in front of me. I ran one scenario after another through my mind, not settling on anything solid. Brody left me alone to contemplate. She probably saw smoke coming out of my ears and knew not to disturb my cranky mind at work. I needed her involved though. She was the computer whiz and the one with a direct line to the FBI. She was also just as smart, if not smarter, than I.

"What do you think if I become buddies with Banner?" I asked her.

"How do you intend to do that?"

"We know he drinks beer," I said. "He loves to hunt. I can be a beer drinking hunter that lives on the other side of the mountain. Get invited to his camp. Invite him over here. Go out into the woods together."

"In order to accomplish what?" she asked.

"Get him talking," I said. "Record him admitting to murder."

"Before you do that," she said. "I need to tell you something. I called David again. They won't come to get the bullet, but they'll test it if we get it to them. Find out if it has Pop's DNA, or Banner's or both."

"If we collect it and take it to the FBI it will be worthless as evidence," I said.

"It's probably already worthless," she said. "Stuck in a tree for so long."

"Maybe the tree protected it from the elements," I suggested.

"So now we're back to digging the thing out, take care not to contaminate it any further, and get it to D.C."

"Do you think Bowdich might apply some pressure on the Sheriff if the bullet is positive for Pop's DNA?"

"I can't say what he might do," she said. "But we're spinning wheels right now. It's worth a shot."

"Let's go back up there tomorrow."

If felt good to be back in the woods. We were both well-rested for the climb and fed up with dealing with the cops. We basked in the earthy smells and all the sights and sounds of the mountain. We enjoyed the time together and took pleasure in the hike, until we closed in on the weed farm. It was time to get serious again. We went through our safety procedure and secured the area. Someone had been up there. Footprints were scattered in the dirt between the rocks, especially near the pot plants. I assumed Banner had come to check on his crop. We both listened intently for sounds of movement in the direction of his camp but heard nothing.

I pulled our ladder out of the weeds and Brody helped me lug it over to the tree in question. She unslung the rifle and stood guard while I went up and located what we hoped was our bullet. I had a small ax and a good hunting knife to extricate it with, assuming it wasn't very deep in the trunk. I hacked and dug until the hole was big enough to peer into. I could see the backside of a rifle round. It was deep enough to present a challenge, but not an insurmountable one.

Before I got too close I put on latex gloves. I had tweezers in a plastic bag in my pocket. We had boiled the tweezers and wiped them down thoroughly. I hacked and dug a little more. Finally, I put the tweezers in the hole and grasped the bullet. It wouldn't budge. I tried working it back and forth but that was hopeless. I went back to the ax, and then the knife.

I resorted to using the ax as a hammer and the knife as a chisel to be more exact. The knife would need a good turn on a grindstone when I was done, but that was the least of my worries. I also had to be careful not to scratch the damn thing. We may need it to undergo ballistics testing. I couldn't mar its natural striations. The tree itself was an old growth elm. The wood was hard, but not like oak. A few of its leaves had begun to turn. There was a light blanket of them on the ground below. Beads of sweat popped out on my brow and dripped into my eyes. Working from the ladder didn't make it any easier. I'd bashed an ugly and obvious scar into the tree just under where a big branch met the trunk.

I made the hole big enough to get the knife wedged in between the bullet and the tree. I cut and jabbed and wiggled all around it until it was loose. Using the tweezers, I gently tugged it out of its resting place and plopped it into the tweezer bag. We had it. I was coming down when I got a warning from Brody.

"Someone's coming," she whispered. "Move."

I watched as she assumed a prone position behind a rock, aiming the rifle towards the approaching sounds. I scrambled down and lowered the ladder as quietly as I could.

"Go, go," she urged.

I dragged the ladder thirty feet or so until it was in tall grass. I checked to make sure I was in possession of all of my tools.

"Come on," I whispered back to her. "Let's beat it."

I hadn't heard a thing. I'd been too busy concentrating on the bullet. Thank God Brody was alert. We rushed down over the first ridge until we made the cover of the thicker trees. Unless the intruder walked far enough to look down this side of the hill, he couldn't see us. We slowed our movements and picked our way deeper into concealment.

"Is it Banner," whispered Brody.

"Can't really tell," I answered. "Doesn't matter. Move carefully and quietly. Just get lower down the mountain. I've got your six."

We managed to extract ourselves without being detected. I worried about the fresh open wound on the tree that I'd created. I worried that the ladder wasn't concealed well enough, but there'd been no time. I'd done what I could. We maintained our noise discipline all the way down the mountain. Not until we approached our cabin did we speak.

"That was a close one," Brody said.

"Could have been bad if you hadn't heard him coming," I said. "Good job."

"I did what you taught me," she said. "I amped up my senses somehow. I can get better at it given enough experience."

"You're awesome," I said. "I can't say how much I appreciate your awesomeness."

"You're not so bad yourself," she said. "I think I'll keep you."

We had the bullet. It was in a zip lock bag along with a pair of boiled tweezers. The next step was to deliver it to the FBI in D.C. No way I was putting it in the mail or sending it via FedEx. We'd have to make the drive and deliver it in person. I hated Washington and everything about it, but we had no other option. I also had to accept the fact that Brody's ex had agreed to help us, for reasons I didn't quite understand. I knew he wouldn't help me if I was alone. I'd have to be careful about his interest in my girl. She was everything to me these days. There was a time, not so long ago, that my old trawler was the only thing I cared about in life. It took precedent over lovers more than once. It was my life and my love. That old boat had taken care of me through thick and thin. We'd shared so many fantastic experiences. When we were underway, we were one. I spoke to her, and she spoke back. Some really fantastic women had played second fiddle to her. I was to blame for that, but that's the way it was. I couldn't imagine a woman ever being more important than that old boat until Brody came along. I'd been a broken soul. My capacity to love was limited. Before Brody, the boat always came first. I didn't have enough to give to support a real and intimate relationship too.

That all changed, but not overnight. Brody was a good sport living the minimalistic life with me. She didn't complain, but eventually, she started hinting at wanting something more. We went back and forth over the idea of buying a nicer, newer boat. I resisted, of course. We went and looked at several candidates. She loved them all, but I always found some reason why they weren't good enough to replace what we already had. She kept her patience with me. It was in my mind that buying a better boat was a betrayal to *Leap of Faith*. I affectionately called her *Miss Leap*. When the idea of a cabin in the woods popped into my mind, it seemed like a reasonable compromise. *Miss Leap* would understand if we bought a house. She wouldn't be happy if we bought a better boat.

That's how we ended up in the Blue Ridge Mountains of North Carolina. The move couldn't have worked out better or come at a better time. I saw us living out our lives there in loving solitude. Brody had her nicer accommodations, better than any old boat. I'd made what for me was the ultimate sacrifice in order to make her happy, but I was happy too. I loved our new cabin. I loved the mountain and the woods. Things couldn't have been better, except for Banner.

FBI Headquarters was four-hundred miles away from our idyllic cabin in the woods. It was a thousand light-years from the life that we'd been living. The drive took us six and a half hours. I didn't like the feel of the place. The last time we were here, the director himself, Chris Wray, ordered Brody to return to duty. She had a clear choice, a respectable career that she'd always wanted, or me. She chose me. I couldn't have blamed her if she chose to return to the Bureau. Actually, I was surprised by her decision.

Director Wray and his associates were not happy with her decision. She had damaging information that they didn't trust her with. We didn't give a shit about the politics or the current climate in Washington. We just wanted to be left alone. Brody's ex-lover was a new element to the situation. He wasn't involved in our previous escapade with the FBI. I wasn't thrilled about working with him, but it was all we had. Bringing them evidence that we'd collected was all sorts of out of bounds. If he wanted to put himself out on a limb on our behalf, I had to accept his help, even though it put him and Brody into close proximity.

I couldn't ignore his motive to get closer to her, but I hoped to use him to further my cause. I had to be secure in my relationship with Brody to pull it off. His affinity for her could work to our advantage, or I could lose everything I'd gained by making her happy. I told myself our relationship was safe. I couldn't believe anything else. We trusted each other. Now was not the time to break that agreement.

Twelve

We checked into a hotel and made arrangements to meet Bowdich the following day. The meeting took place in the lobby of another hotel a few blocks away. The FBI honcho was accompanied by a junior staffer, who took our evidence bag and left immediately.

"I assume you've looked into our suspect since we last talked," Brody said. "Tell us what you've learned."

"His Army file suggests borderline psychopath," he said. "As a civilian, he's nothing more than a lowlife with a few minor infractions."

"He's got plenty of protection from the law," she said. "Father and grandfather sit in high places."

"I was just picking up hints of that," he said. "None of it has come to the attention of the Bureau. Not on our radar."

"I'd appreciate it if you'd delve a little deeper into Senator Banner's history," she said. "We've heard the term Mountain Mafia."

"New one on me," he said. "But sure, I'll poke around a bit."

"What else about Cody?" she asked.

"Here's the file," he said, handing her a manila envelope. Address, date of birth, last known place of employment, prior arrests and convictions. Just a hillbilly struggling to get by. Blows off steam now and then."

"He's a cold-blooded killer," I said. "I've got the photos and the bullet to prove it."

"But local law enforcement couldn't care less," said Brody. "We got a rather stern warning about sticking our nose where it doesn't belong."

"From the law?" he asked.

"Indirectly," she said. "The Banner Elk Police Chief sent an envoy, off the record. He wasn't threatening in the least, just filled us in on what we're up against."

"The Watauga County Sheriff threw us out of his office," I added.

"The two of you think you know what happened, but no one will look into your allegations," he said. "Even with pictures and the bullet."

"They wouldn't look for the bullet nor take it from us if we found it," I said. "Not one member of law enforcement has gone up that mountain to sniff around."

"The pot plants still grow?"

"I've got Banner on camera watering them," I said. "I know for a fact that he didn't plant them. The man he killed planted them."

"I can see why you're frustrated," he said. "I'm not sure how I can help from here."

"Get the DNA results from the bullet," said Brody. "You'll need to match them with Pop Sutton and Cody Banner."

"We've got Banner's from his Army stint," he said. "What happened to the victim's body?"

"Watauga County Morgue," I said. "That's all we know. He does have a sister somewhere in the area though. She may know."

"I'll track down the sister and try to find the body," he said. "Give me some valid reason why we should step in on this case."

"Run Banner's DNA through the various databases," she said. "There's a chance he's killed before but it's an unsolved case. Might be all you need."

"Excellent idea," Bowdich said. "You'd make a great agent."

"I'm still a great agent," she said. "So is Breeze. We're helping you solve a cold case maybe. Now help us solve ours."

There was nothing further to say. Bowdich seemed impressed with what we'd done so far, maybe enough to do some extra digging into the nonsense that was going on in western North Carolina with Senator Banner. Brody's idea that Cody's DNA may be floating around the databases in an unsolved case was brilliant, though probably a longshot. We spent another night at the hotel before driving back to the cabin.

Banner worked at a lumber mill in Roan Mountain. The pay was poor, hence the ratty trailer and rusty truck. The hunting camp was owned by the Senator and included close to a hundred acres of land. Pop's pot farm was not on the Banner property, nor mine. It was in No-Man's-Land like Pop had said. There was a lot of land in the region that really wasn't owned by anyone. Some of that had been claimed by the state for parks and conservation, but not on McGuire Mountain. Pop's claim to his plot of earth was as good as anyone's.

I decided that making myself into a deer hunter was the way to get to Banner. I studied the boundaries of my plot of land. I decided to build a deer stand as close to Banner's property as I could, somewhere along his path to the pot farm. He'd have to check it out. He'd want to know who built it. He'd want to know who else was up there hunting. I'd run into him or he'd come to me sooner or later. I didn't know much about building deer stands, but how hard could it be? I'd already mastered the art of ladder building. I decided I could use that ladder for another stand, closer to the weed.

Brody and I loaded up with tools and weapons and headed up the mountain first thing in the morning. It was a lot to carry. We were in no particular hurry so we stopped and rested whenever we felt the need. We didn't attempt to maintain sound discipline on the way up. We didn't care if we were heard. We were out building tree stands in preparation for the upcoming hunting season. We did stay aware. We listened intently to the woods. Half a mile below the pot farm, we took a new route over towards the Banner property. The undergrowth was thick, almost impassable. I longed for a machete. We found a small clearing that overlooked the obvious trail that Banner took to the weed. It was well within our own property. There was no reason we couldn't put up a stand there. It would piss Banner off to see a stand so close to his property though.

We got to work cutting branches down, trimming them, and chopping them into stair-sized pieces. We nailed them to a tree trunk until we could climb to the first set of branches. We laid longer pieces from branch to branch and nailed them into place. Our work formed a small platform that was sturdy enough to stand or sit on. It was roughly fifteen feet above the ground. It provided a nice view in all directions, but most of the surrounding terrain was too thick to see through. When the leaves all fell in another month, it would provide a much better view.

The first one went up pretty fast. We had time to backtrack and head towards where we'd hidden the ladder. I dragged it even further down the hill and away from the weed farm. We propped it up against a giant oak and drove a few nails through it to secure it in place. It didn't come close to reaching the lowest limbs of the tree. We cut some more ladder rung pieces and I went back up to nail them to the trunk above the ladder. I managed to create steps to the first low limbs. Again we built a small platform in the elbow of the limbs. It was really high up, probably too high, but it gave me a clear view of the weed plants, while still offering some concealment. I could climb up there with my rifle and see everything that was going on at the pot farm.

The work wore us out and we still had to climb back down the mountain, so we packed up our gear and began the descent.

"You okay?" I asked Brody.

"Just tired," she said. "I'll be fine."

We stopped half-way down to rest.

"You want to go deer hunting?" I asked. "We've got two stands."

"I was never into killing innocent animals," she said. "Deer are so pretty."

"And tasty," I said. "But I haven't hunted since I was maybe twenty. Never felt the need. I was raised to hunt. All my friends were avid hunters. I stayed home and accepted some venison whenever it was offered. Ducks and geese too."

"If you are going to try to get in tight with Banner, you're probably going to have to kill a deer or two."

"No doubt," I said. "I'm trying to remember the last time I field dressed a deer."

"Might want to brush up on that if you want to pass for a hunter," she said.

"I remember watching my dad the first time," I said. "Grossed me out, but I was just a boy."

"Did you have a good relationship with your father?"

"I loved my dad," I said. "He was a great role model for me, but hard to follow."

"How so?"

"He was bigger than life," I said. "Had everyone's respect. A man's man. He was tough as nails but everyone loved him. Military, law enforcement, discipline. I had my rebellious stage. I didn't want to only be my father's son. I wanted to make my own way, but I'm still proud to have had him as my dad. He taught me to be a man without causing me to turn on him. I just had to learn to deal with his legacy."

"Sounds like a father to be proud of."

"I miss him sometimes," I admitted. "You would've liked him. He would've liked you."

"Neither of your parents are alive are they?"

"Nope," I said. "Lost my sister too."

"You've always got me," she said.

"And I'm grateful for that," I said. "You ready?"

"Let's get home."

Back at the cabin, we turned on the TV to learn about Hurricane Florence. The Category Four storm was headed directly for North Carolina. We were a long way from the coast and high up in the mountains so I wasn't worried but figured we better keep an eye on things as they developed. I pitied the people on the coast.

One year prior, we'd had a battle with Hurricane Irma. We worked hard to prepare out boat and anchor it as safely as possible. We'd intended to stay in a condo nearby until a mandatory evacuation order was issued. We fled north but couldn't find a hotel that wasn't full until we reached Charleston, South Carolina. Remnants of the storm ended up flooding that city and knocking out power. We lived like refugees for three days until we could escape and return to Florida. Both trips, up and back, were chaotic and miserable. We found our boat still floating and breathed a sigh of relief. It took weeks to get her back in shape afterward. I didn't want to deal with another hurricane. Moving to the mountains was supposed to keep us far removed from them.

We still had several days to prepare for the worst. We started watching the Weather Channel. It looked like our real concern would be excessive rainfall. We'd probably lose power, but we had a generator and enough fuel to last for a few days. I walked the property with an eye on the creek and how high it might get. There was no way its waters could get into the house, but they might reach the garage underneath. There was a big culvert under the road coming in that looked vulnerable to flood conditions. If it washed out we'd be stuck at the cabin until it could be fixed.

We took stock of our supplies and decided to load up on necessities. We still didn't know if the storm would impact us or not, but we wanted to be ready if it did. We didn't want to wait until the last minute when things like water and food staples would be sold out at the local stores. I grabbed some extra toilet paper while we were shopping too.

Over the next few days, the forecasters all came into agreement as to the track of the storm. The center of the cone of death was

Wilmington, North Carolina. There was talk of it coming ashore as a Cat Four and stalling inland, dumping ridiculous amounts of rain over several days. We seemed to be on the outer edge of that scenario. We'd still get a lot of rain, but no storm force winds. I kept surveying our property to see where all that water might go. The laws of nature and physics told me that it had to continue down the mountain. I didn't think the creek would bother the cabin.

I started making scouting trips prior to the opening of deer season. I found new ground that I hadn't traveled before. I'd always just headed straight for Pop's old hangout since the day I'd met him. I rarely saw a deer while moving through the woods. If I sat still for a decent amount of time, they'd come to me. I didn't sit in the deer stands. I wanted to avoid tainting them with my scent. I wanted them to blend in with the natural landscape. They'd be there when I needed them.

I saw doe after doe on my excursions. The mountain was full of them. If we ever really needed the meat, it would be no trouble to take a female deer. To prove my abilities to Banner, I'd need to take down a big buck, but I just wasn't seeing them. I told myself that when the Rut began, the bucks would come for the females. Meanwhile, I identified known routes of travel and grazing spots for the deer that were already there.

Down the mountain at the cabin, they came to my apple trees almost every day. The trees were heavy with fruit and dropped plenty of snacks to the ground to provide the deer with easy pickings. I vaguely remembered some old farmer's belief that a heavy fruit crop was a sign of a cold winter. Down in Banner Elk, they looked to the wooly worm to determine the winter forecast. Brody wanted to go to the Wooly Worm Festival in October.

I was really getting to know my turf. The rock and wood that surrounded me felt as much like home as the sand and water had before. I enjoyed taking it all in. I'd sit quietly, waiting for a deer, and allow the sights and sounds to embrace me. I always heard the deer before I saw it, without fail. I tried to smell them coming, but they smelled like the woods. If I concealed myself well, they would get within a few yards of me without being spooked. I felt as comfortable in the woods as the deer themselves. If it wasn't for our sweet little cabin and Brody, I would have set up a shelter and sleep up there.

That thought made me want to search for Pop's shelter. If I could find it, I could use it as a base of operations for overnight trips. I might learn more about how the man survived his harsh mountain environment, or about the man himself. It was too late that day to search for it, but I vowed to find it soon. Besides, it was always great to return home to Brody. She had dinner cooking when I got back. She looked radiant in jeans and a flannel shirt. I could still picture her in a bikini on a beach in Florida. We'd come a long way and made a major change, but it agreed with us both.

"I'm going to find Pop's shelter," I told her.

"Any particular reason?" she asked.

"I have the distinct feeling that however this ends with Banner, it's going to happen up there," I said. "I need to be better on the mountain than him. Pop was the master of the mountain. I can learn some things."

"You plan to spend nights up there?"

"A few, when the time comes," I said. "I've got to find it first."

"Can I help you look?"

"That'd be great," I said. "Let me know when you're ready."

"I get a little bored when you're gone all day," she said. "I'm ready when you are."

"Awesome," I said. "Let's start tomorrow."

I was excited to have Brody share the mountain experience with me. This was our new life. I'd immersed myself in it much more so than she had. She'd been a great help finding the bullet. We were a team no matter our surroundings. We set out in search of Pop's home base the next day.

We started from the weed patch. I walked all around the perimeter looking for obvious signs of his comings and goings. Of course, I didn't find anything. I stopped and stood still, feeling the vibrations, letting the mountain speak to me. Which way did he come? I ruled out the direction of Banner's hunting camp. He'd avoid that at all costs. He didn't come from the direction of my cabin. I guessed that he'd want to be as far from people as possible. That meant he lived somewhere higher up. I'd never been any higher than the weed farm. It was not friendly terrain. I tried to look through the trees up the slope. I couldn't see much. I figured he wouldn't want to be too far from the creek. He had to camp above us, but not too far.

I told Brody to look for some access going up, somewhere the brush wasn't too thick to move through. We split up and probed the perimeter of the semi-flat plot of land we were standing on. It took a while, but we finally decided on a path. It ascended sharply but had plenty of rock and root footholds. We carefully climbed a hundred feet or so, until we saw what might have been a trail off to our left. It was a narrow and low tunnel that disappeared into thick growth. We crawled along a ledge for another fifty feet. Something told me to stop.

"What do you see?" asked Brody.

"Nothing yet," I answered. "I think we're close. It's here somewhere."

I let the mountain talk to me. I summoned Pop, asking him to direct me. I deployed all of my senses to maximum awareness. I waited for a sign. I closed my eyes and absorbed all incoming feelings. When I opened them, I saw a wall of dying greenery. Upon close inspection, I saw that it wasn't natural. It had been cut and carefully placed. This had to be the place. I pointed it out to Brody and we crawled towards the wall of cut evergreens. I poked around until I found an easily movable branch. Behind the façade was a semi-cave, Pop's hideout. It was too dark to see much. We didn't bring a flashlight.

I brought Brody in behind me and let my eyes adjust to the dimness.

Thirteen

It took several minutes before we could see anything at all. I was glad to find an oil lamp pushed up against the back wall. Attached to it with a thin strip of deer hide was a grill lighter. I dialed the wick up a tad and lit the lamp. We had light, and I assumed it put off some heat as well. The little cave was not what I had expected. There was a decent bedroll up under a ledge of rock about the size of a coffin. There were two plastic containers with lids holding some of Pop's belongings. One held books and the other was full of small tools, silverware, a can opener and the like.

There were several books about Pop's father, Popcorn Sutton, including **Popcorn Sutton; The Making and Marketing of a Hillbilly Hero**. There was also one written by Popcorn himself called **Me and My Likker**. There were several books on the history of the Blue Ridge and Smokey Mountains. Underneath all of them was a writing notebook, the kind one uses to keep a journal. I opened it up and read the title at the top of the first page; **Denying a Legacy**, by Marvin Sutton.

Stacked in a corner were a pot and pan, along with some utensils. In a plastic garbage bag, we found thick winter clothes and a down jacket. Above us was the tarp Pop had described to me. Hanging from one of the hooks was the travel rod I'd given him. I took it down and handed it to Brody.

"I might as well get some use out of it," I said.

"You should read his memoir too," she said. "If it's any good we should try to get it published."

"Excellent idea," I said.

The tarp was situated so that water dripped off near the entrance to the lair. There was a Mason jar under it to catch the water. A small trench carried the excess out away from the living space, what little there was. The lamp had already started to warm up the interior. Pop had lived a minimal existence, but he was far from homeless. I couldn't imagine being stuck in there for days on end during a snowstorm. His well-worn reading material and his journal looked to be his only form of entertainment.

The only other supplies evident were some canned goods and other nonperishable foods. We could survey his entire house without taking a step. I wondered how I could best use it to my advantage. I doubted Banner would try to harvest his crop in the dark, but he might arrive at first light. I could be there waiting if that time ever came. What would I do if it did?

I backed out of the cave and onto the small ledge outside. I continued along the ledge instead of going back the way we came. Soon I came to Pop's kitchen. It was a small rock formation with a metal grate over it and the cold remains of a fire. Twigs and thin branches were piled nearby. I pictured him crawling over here with a pan of soup or the meat from some small game and cooking it after dark. I hadn't noticed any hides or furs inside his home. He must have had another place to stash them.

I crawled back to where Brody was waiting. The sky was gray and there was a chill in the air. She was ready to go home. I was good with that. We'd found what we'd come to find. I knew that Pop wouldn't mind that I'd invaded his private space. He was probably proud of me for finding it. Before we started back down, I motioned for Brody to pause. I used hand signals to tell her to listen to the mountain. We needed to be sure that no one had come up to the pot farm before we backtracked through it.

We both tuned in our senses. We concentrated on the sights, sounds, smells and even vibrations all around us. Squirrels, chipmunks, and birds made their presence known. Leaves rustled in the breeze. Clouds rolled over our heads from east to west. Fog was settling in on the higher elevations. Neither of us detected anything human other than ourselves. It was safe to work our way down.

We didn't make it back to the cabin until after dark. There was no warm meal cooking. I got a fire going while Brody started dinner. I propped the fly rod in a corner and dusted off Pop's memoir. His grammar and sentence composition were surprisingly good. His handwriting was a blocky plain script, not cursive. It was clear and readable. I thumbed through the pages and noticed that sometimes the ink was black, but sometimes it was blue. Where does a vagrant get a new pen? (Wherever he can).

The first chapter was an effort to explain the difference between loving his father, and not wanting to be like him. It was clear that Pop was torn about his feelings for his dad. Popcorn had possessed an exuberant personality that many folks loved, but some hated. Pop was proud to see his father enjoy a certain amount of fame, but he didn't like what the fame did to him. The boy was not the most important thing in the old moonshiner's life. Apparently being a father to his children wasn't on Popcorn's priority list. Pop resented that. There was a sister who felt the same way. The two siblings separated from their father and made their own way in life at an early age.

I stopped reading and walked back through what we knew so far. I tried to prioritize what needed to be done next. We still hadn't heard from the FBI concerning the bullet we'd recovered.

"I think we should break out that SAT phone and call your boyfriend," I told Brody.

"Jealousy doesn't become you," she replied. "One the other hand, they should have run the evidence by now."

"Let's see what they've got," I said.

Bowdich answered Brody right away. She put the phone on speaker.

"Pop's remains were cremated," he said. "Nothing incriminating on Banner yet, but we're still working on a few things."

"We just so happened to discover a trove of the deceased's personal belongings," she told him. "I'm sure his DNA is in the mix."

"You realize none of this is admissible in court?" he said. "We're way out of bounds here."

"We just need to be certain that Banner is the killer," she explained. "It may have a bearing on what actions we take in the future."

"Not sure I like the sound of that," said Bowdich.

"But you got a second person's DNA off the bullet?" she asked.

"There was enough trace biological matter to discern DNA," he said. "Contamination may have rendered it useless, but we won't know until we get a sample to compare it to."

"Trace isn't good enough for a proper comparison," she said. "At least not on what I provide you. You need a skin scraping or a hair, right?"

"A hair would work," he said. "But we have to know that it came from the deceased. A defendant's lawyer will kill us."

"They can object all they want," she said. "But the jury will still see and hear the evidence."

"Not if a judge throws it out," he countered. "We wouldn't attempt to take this to trial on what we have."

"So we lay it all out for the Sheriff here," she said. "If he won't follow up then you lean on him, hard. Threats from the Bureau can be quite effective, as you know."

"You're asking an awful lot here," he said. "Unpaid lab testing, influencing a local investigation, tampering with evidence."

"We've kept our mouths shut over what the Bureau did to us," she reminded him. "We could be very wealthy by now if we had squeaked enough. You and your boys would have too much explaining to do and your reputation would likely be lost forever."

"I wouldn't advise taking that route," he said. "We have a truce over the matter, but this hints at blackmail."

"A truce but not a written contract," she said. "I don't want to betray the FBI. I'm simply asking for your help."

"Get me a good DNA medium," he said. "We'll run it. I'll let you know."

"We'll be in touch," she said.

The conversation was much less friendly than previous ones. We may have pushed him a bit too hard. I trusted that Brody knew what she was doing. She knew the inner workings of the FBI and she also knew Bowdich. I chose not to waste time dissecting what I'd just heard.

"We'll go find what we need tomorrow," I said. "As long as his hair and beard were, it shouldn't be a problem."

"Another drive to Washington," she said. "Probably for nothing."

"We're making progress," I told her. "How long did it take you to find me?"

"Too long," she said. "You were a worthy adversary."

"Just like I'll be for Banner," I declared.

"But I found you in the end," she said.

"Only after I'd been cleared," I said. "If I was still wanted I wouldn't have been sitting in that bar. You would have gotten close, but not close enough."

"Fair point," she said. "But I did find you."

"Outstanding detective work and perseverance," I said. "Made me curious about you the minute we met."

"I was curious about you for a year before we met," she said. "I didn't understand how a boat bum could avoid the reach of the FBI. I had no idea you were so resourceful and so far off the grid. People just don't live like that."

"You'd be surprised," I said. "Florida has an embarrassment of fugitives."

"Homeless and drug-addicted mostly," she said. "You were neither."

"I had a boat and a booze problem instead," I said. "But I managed to keep my wits."

"You're a unique individual, Breeze," she said. "I'm honored to share this life with you."

"I thank the good Lord daily for you, Brody," I said. "I hardly deserve a woman like you."

"Deserve has nothing to do with it," she said. "We were meant for each other."

"Which is why you're humoring me on this Pop and Banner thing," I said. "Thanks for understanding."

"Now that I'm part of the mission," she said. "I want to get that son of a bitch as much as you do."

"Music to my ears," I said.

The next day we packed two flashlights and a pair of tweezers that had been sterilized and placed in a ziplock bag. We made a beeline for Pop's lair, only stopping briefly to listen to the woods. Once inside the cave, we each searched one half of the tiny space. It didn't take long. Brody plucked a long gray hair with the tweezers and placed it carefully in the bag. We backed out of there and started down towards the weed farm, but someone was down there.

I motioned for Brody to stop and hold still. We both froze and listened. I couldn't see so I carefully crawled a little further along the ledge. I didn't make a sound as I got into position. I slowly parted two branches to get a look below. Banner was walking among the plants. He had his rifle slung over his shoulder and a fifth of whiskey in his hand. He took a slug from the bottle and inspected his crop. The plants weren't ready to harvest yet. I gathered that he knew as much.

I watched as he crossed over the plot towards my side of the mountain. He poked around, looking for footprints or other signs that someone else had been up there. We hadn't been particularly careful on our way through. No doubt we'd left tracks here and there. He saw something that made him unsling his weapon. He assumed a cautious stance, looking around. I eased back away from my vantage point, motioning to Brody to retreat. We were vulnerable without a rifle. We were on a narrow ledge with nowhere to run. We weren't prepared to have a standoff with Banner. I silently cursed myself for my stupidity. There was nothing else to do but hide. I looked Brody in the eye then transferred my gaze to Pop's den. She understood. We crawled back to the entrance and slithered inside. I repositioned the blocking branches to conceal the cave. It was dark but we made no effort to create light. I touched Brody on the shoulder and made downward hand motions.

"Stay calm," I whispered. "Lower your heart rate. Listen and be still."

We could hear him stomping around below us. The spot where we climbed off the plateau with the weed plants was solid rock. He wouldn't see our tracks going upward. He had to be baffled about the mystery person who knew about this place. The body had disappeared first, now someone had been here walking around. Nothing was disturbed but his peace of mind. It would be a real head-scratcher for him. We listened as he walked away from the ledge towards our side of the mountain. The sounds grew faint, then stopped. Banner spoke loudly, almost yelling. "Whoever you are, let's talk," he said. "I gather you know where to find me."

Getting no reply, he walked back through the weed plants and started down the slope towards his hunting camp. We remained still and silent for a long time. I thought he might settle in and wait us out. It's what I would have done. He was familiar with these woods and had the patience of a hunter. I pictured him lying in concealment, listening and watching for us. I thought I could slip out undetected, but I wasn't confident that Brody could do the same. The cave walls closed in on us in the dark. It was uncomfortable in more ways than one.

"Stay here," I whispered. "I'm going to go out and get a feel for what's going on."

I crawled out on the ledge and sat cross-legged with my back to the rock face. I slowed my breathing and relaxed. I felt my heart beating slower and slower. The sounds came into focus. I smelled the mountain air. There was a hint of gun oil and leather on the wind. The creek babbled down the mountain like it always did. A crow was raising hell somewhere in the distance. There was no indication that Banner was still close.

I further dropped my resistance and let the increased flow of information wash over me. The sounds became more and more clear. The smells introduced themselves one by one. I felt the vibrations of a hummingbird in the treetops. I could see the breeze, not just feel it. Banner was gone. Nothing about the sensations that I experienced told me that he was waiting for us to show ourselves.

Just then I heard a sound that was not part of nature. It was a beer can being opened. There was no doubt what I'd heard, even though the hunting cabin was a mile away. I'd heard the sound millions of time. The suddenness of it snapped me out of my hyper-aware state. I pulled myself back to normal and went to get Brody.

"It's safe to come out now," I said. "He's back at his shack."

"How can you be sure?"

"I heard him crack open a beer," I told her. "If you want to try to hear it I'm sure he'll open another one soon."

"Let's just get out of here," she said. "We got what we came for."

Over the next few days, we got the hair sample to Bowdich in Washington. We met at a different hotel but the procedure was the same. An evidence tech took our baggie and disappeared.

"There is trace on the bullet," he said. "But we can't make certain it was Banner's until we have his weapon and can run ballistics."

"If at some point someone decides to talk to the man, maybe get a warrant, then maybe you could get his gun," said Brody.

"A lot of dots would have to be connected before that would ever happen," he said. "At least from our standpoint."

"From our standpoint," she said. "We're drowning you with evidence. You and the Sheriff both."

"We have a different point of view," he said. "Just so you know, we're starting to learn a few things about your senator. Not exactly mountain mafia stuff."

"Just run of the mill corruption?" I asked.

"The same things go on all around the country every day," he said. "He runs his little fiefdom until the voters take him out or he dies. Small potatoes."

"Until it comes to covering up a murder," I said. "Not the senator himself, but officers of the law under his thumb."

"We're still learning about him," he said. "But it's not a high priority."

"Let us know if the hair matches what's on the bullet," said Brody.

"SAT phone?" he asked.

"Send a text," she said. "We'll get it when we turn it on."

I'd been to Washington three times to deal with the FBI. Each time I wanted a hot shower afterward. The town reeked of sleaze. Bowdich was barely tolerating us. The North Carolina authorities were ignoring us. Pop's death wouldn't be avenged in any meaningful way. That's the part that really bothered me. I didn't give a shit about the weed. I didn't care about a state senator handing out favors or taking kickbacks. I really didn't even care about police departments that didn't do a great job-solving crimes or prosecuting criminals. Pop's life meant something to me, though. In a short period of time, he'd made an impact on me. His ability to live completely off the grid and isolated from society seemed like a noble pursuit to me. It had once been my life's goal. Brody had changed that and I was good with it, but Pop had persisted, alone in the wilderness.

I thought about how lonely his existence must have been. I knew a little something about being alone. The bad shit didn't happen when I stayed to myself. Only when I involved myself with other people did things start to go wrong. My problem was an affinity for pretty women. I was drawn out of hiding whenever I encountered a woman who intrigued me. It inevitably led to trouble. I knew I could avoid that by staying by myself, but I simply couldn't resist. My relationship with Brody had survived the storm. We left our old life behind to live alone, but together. It seemed like the perfect solution, but here we were embroiled in yet another mess.

Fourteen

Brody was getting more comfortable in the woods so we decided to purchase a second hunting rifle. We alternated days exploring the mountain and tending to cabin chores. We steered clear of the crime scene and the two stands we had built. Brody was learning to listen more closely to her senses, but she hadn't elevated the art to the moments of Zen that I'd experienced.

I found a way to sneak up on Banner's shack without coming down the mountain the same way he did. We made occasional forays to observe the place, using our scopes to get a long-range view. There was no new obvious activity, but deer season was still a ways off.

Hurricane Florence threatened to climb the mountains and dump a ton of rain on us, but that threat never materialized. We never lost power and no trees fell during the event. The creek got a little livelier and the sky was dark gray for two days. We were lucky. Millions on the coast were less fortunate. After the remnants of the storm passed out of our region, the sun returned and life went on as normal.

Bowdich texted Brody to tell us that the DNA on the bullet was likely a match for Pop Sutton, but there was enough tree matter to keep the percentage below what was an absolute certainty. The same applied to identifying the other trace as Banner's. What little they recovered was diluted with plant DNA. Who knew plants had DNA? The basic building blocks of life are the same in both plants and animals, at the structural level. A prosecuting attorney would tell the jury that a match was made, with ninety percent certainty. A defense attorney would tell them that wasn't good enough. He'd introduce reasonable doubt, not that this evidence would ever make it to trial.

In the court of my mind, Cody Banner was guilty of murder. Judge Breeze would eventually preside over his sentencing hearing, or see to it that a real judge did.

An opportunity to introduce myself to Banner presented itself. I was walking towards the tree stand we'd built that bordered his property when I heard him coming. I froze at first and listened to his progress up the hill. When he got close enough I called out.

"Yo, another man on the mountain," I yelled.

It was his turn to freeze, but he responded soon enough.

"Who's there?" he said.

"A neighbor out doing some scouting," I told him. "Look up about ten feet and scan the trees. There's a homemade tree stand on this side of the line. I'll meet you there."

We stood face to face under the stand. He was suspicious but he tried to cover it with a friendly smile.

"The name's Breeze," I said, not offering my hand. "I live down the other side."

"Banner," he said. "This stand is damn close to our land."

"I realize that," I admitted. "But the doe are walking through here most mornings. Figured I could pick one off before it made it to your ground. Or that a big buck will be trailing them when it gets cooler."

"You've been up here scouting a lot then," he said. "You been up on the plateau above here?"

"I've got a real good idea where my land ends," I said. "I've tried to stay within what's mine, but I understand that no one owns the land higher up."

"My family has been hunting it for generations," he said. "Not a legal claim, but folks around here recognize it."

"I'm new to the area," I said. "Don't know many folks yet."

"Welcome to the mountains," he said. "Mind your own, and you'll get along okay."

"I intend to do just that," I said. "Just wanted to make you aware of my presence up here, for safety's sake and all."

"You got more stands up here?" he asked.

"One, down below that ridge you mentioned," I said. "It overlooks no man's land."

"I don't travel that side of the hill," he said. "Shouldn't be an issue."

"Not that I need your permission," I said.

His eyes told me that he didn't like his authority challenged. This mountain was probably the only place where he considered himself the boss. I was the interloper. He was also trying to juggle my presence with the mystery person who'd been walking around his pot plants and the disappearing body. Coming out in the open to introduce myself didn't seem like a thing that person would do. I looked him directly in the eye and awaited his response.

"I tell you what, neighbor," he said. "I'll be hosting a pre-opening day cookout at my cabin. We'll throw some meat on the grill and drink a bunch of beer with my boys. It's kind of a tradition to kick off the season. You're invited, but no women allowed. Friday before opening day around six."

"Which driveway is yours?"

"Before you get to the church," he said. "Just two tire tracks in the grass. No gate."

"I've seen it," I said. "My car won't make it up the hill. I'll have to walk up from the road."

"Wear your orange," he said. "In case one of my buddies gets trigger happy."

"Thanks for the invite," I said. "Good to meet you."

I turned and started walking back the way I came. I didn't walk like smoke. I didn't want to give him an indication of what I was capable of. I was just a dumb city slicker trampling about in the woods. No way was I capable of removing the body or casing his weed. I could hear him snort in derision once he thought I was out of earshot.

I realized that attending his cookout drinking party would come with some risk. Hanging out with some drunk strangers in the mountains didn't appeal to me, but the possibility of getting closer to Banner did. I'd have to be on my toes, stay a few drinks behind and remain wary. I could always bail out at the first sign of animosity. I went home and told Brody what had happened.

"You'll be amongst some real mountain men," she said. "Good old boys who'll view you as an outsider."

"I'll have to play the role," I said. "Make them think I'm serious about hunting."

"Beer, beef, and bucks," she said. "Glad I'm not going."

"Should be interesting."

"Could be dangerous," she said.

"I'm aware of that."

Time moved on with no word from the Sheriff or the FBI. Pop was forgotten by everyone but me. The weed plants continued to grow. The rains from Hurricane Florence gave them some extra juice without damaging them. The early fall temperatures were above normal. It looked to be a lucrative crop come harvest time. I still hadn't seen a buck on the mountain, but the does weren't ready yet. They fattened up on apples and lush greenery in preparation for winter. They never strayed far from the creek. One doe was still leading around two yearlings. I figured the rut would finally relieve her of her motherly duties.

I bought a case of cheap beer to donate to Banner's cookout. I carried my hunting knife openly. I wore boots instead of my hiking shoes. I let my beard go for four days. After parking at the base of the drive, I walked up the steep slope to Banner's shack. I was a little late on purpose. There were four pickups parked in front of the cabin. All had four-wheel drive and faded paint. Two had Tennessee plates and two were from North Carolina. I walked behind them and peered over the tailgates. I saw an assortment of chainsaws, gas cans, tools, and beer cans.

There was a fire going in the pit. Four men sat around the blaze, each with a beer in hand.
"Banner," I said. "I brought reinforcements."
He took the beer and dumped it in an old cow trough full of ice.
"This is Breeze," he said to his pals. "Lives over on the other side. Plans to do some hunting too."
The three friends directed nods and grunts my way.
"Thanks for having me," I said to no one in particular.

I stood there awkwardly for a minute until I saw another chair by the shack. I carried it to the edge of the fire and took a seat.

"I'm Jake," the man to my right said. "This here's Zane and Rob. You get one of the McGuire cabins?"

"That's right," I said. "Right next to the creek."

"Down the bottom of McGuire Mountain Road," said Jake.

"That's me."

"How much land you got to hunt on?" he asked.

"A good chunk of the east face," I said. "Stops just below the plateau."

"We don't go over there," he said. "But we do go up above the ridge."

"I don't plan to go beyond what I've already scouted," I told him. "Only reason for me to be up there would be to track a wounded runner."

"Then you'd be walking our hunting grounds," he warned. "Spooking our deer."

"What do you propose I do in that situation then?"

"Wait till dark," Banner spoke up. "When we're done. Let me know you're going to track it in the morning. We might even help."

I pictured myself in no man's land, followed by men with guns. I didn't like the picture. I couldn't know what Banner had told these men about me.

"I didn't come here to get into a pissing match over hunting grounds," I said. "I came to drink beer and eat some meat."

"I'll fire up the grill," said Banner. "You boys play nice."

I was still on my first beer, but my counterparts were obviously several drinks in. The conversation turned to college football. The Appalachian State team had nearly beaten Penn State to start the season. I learned the proper pronunciation was "App a latch un" as opposed to "App a lay shun." I also learned that real men didn't drive a Subaru. Half the cars on the road were damned hippie granola eating Subarus. Men drove full-sized trucks. The brand didn't matter as long as it was Ford, Chevy, or Dodge. No Jap trucks for them, no sir. I was supposed to be embarrassed by my front-wheel-drive car, but at least it was made in America.

The grill produced hunks of goose wrapped in bacon, along with a slab of venison roast. We all hacked at the roast with our knives and ate with our fingers. I washed my hands with beer and wiped them on my pants. I grabbed another beer and returned to the fire. More logs were added and it sprang to life in the darkness of night. The conversation turned to women. Banner's friends were all married. The wives had all gained weight after childbirth and ceased to be the young hotties they were on their wedding day. The men had developed beer bellies, grown beards, and spent too much time in the woods instead of home with the family. Banner was still single. Apparently, he dated attractive women from time to time, but they all turned out to be crazy.

I was questioned about my better half. I mostly told the truth.
"We're not married," I said. "But we've been together for quite a while. She's still beautiful

and we still have sex on a regular basis. I'm a lucky man in that respect."

"How'd you manage to avoid marriage?" asked Jake. "We all got roped in right out of high school."

"I didn't meet her until I was in my fifties," I said. "We've got it pretty good so we figured why screw it up?"

"Don't buy her a ring," he said. "That's when they start getting fat."

We all laughed at the correlation. The discussion deteriorated from there. Jake liked to spit his chew into the fire. Zane didn't care how loud his farts were. Rob's vocabulary was dominated by cuss words. Banner seemed to be getting comfortably numb in his chair. I guessed that he'd snuck a toke or two during the evening. He stopped Jake from adding more wood to the fire.

"Let her die out," he said. "Big day tomorrow. We should all get some sleep."

I stood up and prepared to leave.

"Good luck guys," I said.

"We're all gonna meet back here around dusk," said Jake. "See who killed what."

"I'll have to drag mine down the other side of the mountain," I said. "If I get done early enough I'll stop in."

I started walking down the steep drive in the dark. I was out of sight of the shack when Banner yelled.

"Get yourself a truck soon, ya hear?" he said. "Like a real man."

I just kept walking, thinking about the night's events. It all seemed pretty typical to me. I'd been to similar gatherings when I was younger, back in Maryland. Banner didn't tip his hand. His friends didn't treat me like an enemy. I caught him looking at me a few times, trying to figure me out. I don't think I gave him anything to be suspicious about. I stood my ground when I needed to, but other than that I acted like one of the guys.

Brody was anxious to hear how it went. I filled her in quickly before hitting the sack for the night. I'd had five beers over the course of three hours or so. That was well within my comfort zone. I threw down a shot of rum as a nightcap before getting in bed. My hunting clothes had been hanging from a tree for days.

Brody had cleaned our weapons while I was gone. We were ready to kill a deer or two.

During the pre-hunt party, there had been a strategy discussion for the first day. Everyone wanted to kill a big buck, of course. The plan was to let the does pass in hopes of a buck's arrival. If they didn't see a buck by late afternoon, they'd take a doe for meat. They didn't want anyone shooting up the woods and spooking the wary males just to kill a small female. I was strongly encouraged to use the same strategy.

Personally, I didn't really want to kill anything, but I felt that I needed to in order to prove my bonafides as a hunter. I'd let the does walk on by gladly, but I couldn't let a buck escape me if I saw one. I didn't have much confidence that I'd get a chance at a buck the first day. I still hadn't seen any on my scouting trips. The weather had remained warm well into fall. The pot plants were flourishing and would soon be ready to harvest.

Brody and I left the cabin before first light. We made it most of the way up the hill before sunrise. I put her in the stand near Banner's turf. I took the stand below the ridge that overlooked the weed. I had a more unobstructed view, but we'd seen the most activity around Brody's stand. She didn't want to shoot a deer either, but she could watch and report to me later if she saw a good one.

As the sun came up over the Blue Ridge, I listened to Banner and his crew disperse on the other side of the mountain. They'd come part of the way together, then split up. They were later to arrive than we were. I swear I could smell the beer on their breath. I sat quietly and enjoyed the coolness of the morning. Within an hour I heard multiple deer coming up from the east. I had my back to them, so I very slowly turned to get a look. The mother with the two yearlings was picking her way between saplings and low brush, headed for the creek. Her ears twitched constantly. She'd take five or six steps then stop and listen. Her young mimicked her movements.

If they went straight for the creek they'd be an easy target. The mother was a big girl that would provide plenty of food, but I didn't particularly want to separate her from the little ones. They'd make their own way soon enough though. I watched as they took an indirect path around a clearing. They stuck to cover and remained alert like they knew someone was watching. They climbed down the bank to get a drink and disappeared from view.

I could no longer hear the other hunters. They'd found their spots and settled down. I couldn't see Brody from where I was, but she was quiet too. There were five humans on the mountain, lying in wait for some poor buck to wander across their path. I saw no other movement for hours. I dozed momentarily with my back against the tree. A cracking twig alerted me. I heard a snort, then a hoof scratching the ground. A buck was very close, but I didn't see him.

He was behind me, coming the same way the doe had traveled. He was on her trail. I did not risk turning to get a look at him. I knew where he was going. I very slowly shifted my rifle, inches at a time. My heart was beating too fast. I needed to get control and be calm. Brody was a fantastic shot with a pistol, but I was better with the long gun. I had a way of slowing my breathing and heart rate until they almost stopped. When I got like that, I was deadly accurate.

I told myself to slow down. I used that Zen-like magic to listen to the buck while lowering my metabolism. I visualized a heart monitor getting slower and slower. I took a breath about six times per minute, slowly. The buck was less graceful than the doe had been. He stayed in the brush, but crashed along, stomping down weeds. He stopped to lift his head and sniff the air. I didn't know if he sensed my presence or if he was locating the doe. It was probably both. He didn't get to be this big by being a dumbass.

My body was ready to shoot. My mind wasn't fully onboard with the idea. I wasn't even sure if I would pull the trigger when I needed to, but I raised the rifle and lined up the scope. My heart rate ticked up a notch when I saw my target. He was the biggest deer I'd seen in North Carolina. I doubted he was any kind of record or anything, but he was a fine specimen. I tried to count the points on his rack. I couldn't decide if it was nine or ten. It didn't matter to me.

I could see the disturbed weeds where the doe had gone down the bank. I moved the weapon to put the scope there and waited. The buck stepped out of the brush and seemed to puff up his neck, a warning to intruders that he was about to get busy. I slid my line of fire slightly to the right until I had his heart in the crosshairs. I had my moment of truth. I smoothly pulled the trigger. The buck went down but he didn't give up. He struggled back to his feet and staggered down the hill. It took a minute to climb down from the stand and pursue him. There was plenty of blood where he'd been hit and more along the way. I peered down over the ridge and saw him standing there, panting hard. The easy thing to do would be to put him down with another shot, but it was poor etiquette. The day's hunt would be over for everyone else.

I started walking down the hill towards him. He tried to run but stumbled. The loss of blood was weakening him. I found him lying in a shallow wash surrounded by tall grass. He was still breathing, but not thrashing about. One foot was pawing the grass slowly. He didn't want to give up, but he was clearly dying. He looked at me with one eye as I stood over him. I had my knife ready but didn't move in yet. One last burst of energy and he could rip me up with his antlers.

The pawing stopped. It was a long time between breaths after that. When I saw my chance, I grabbed one side of his rack and slit his throat with the knife. If he wasn't dead yet, he would be in a few seconds. I stepped back away from my kill. Blood pooled around his neck and chest. There was no more movement. It was done.

I gazed down at what I had wrought with a touch of remorse. He was a majestic creature, only meeting his demise because he was chasing tail. He'd never once shown himself in all the times I'd scouted the mountain. I didn't drink his blood or take a bite out of his heart or any of that silly horseshit you see in the movies. It wasn't my first deer, but it was the first in over three decades. I silently wished him well in the afterlife.

I dragged him away from the pool of blood so I wouldn't have to stand in it. He was damned heavy. I gutted him out then dragged him away from that pile. He was still too much to carry very far. I estimated he weighed close to two-hundred pounds even after being field dressed. I couldn't make it down the mountain carrying Pop's body, and he wasn't much over a hundred pounds. I did, however, have Brody to help this time. I took a minute to regain situational awareness. I made sure no persons or bears were closing in on me before heading towards Brody's tree stand.

When I got close enough I gave a quick whistle so she'd know I was approaching. She climbed down quietly and met me on the doe path.
"Got a big boy," I told her. "I need some help with it."
"Pretty lucky to nail a buck on the first day," she said.

"Right place at the right time," I said. "Thanks to preparation."

"Let's get busy," she said.

Brody was impressed at the size of my kill, but we both knew we had a serious chore in front of us. We decided to build a travois, or drag sled like the Indians used. We didn't have much for tools available other than hunting knives. We poked around in search of usable branches but came up short. I ended up disassembling the ladder to my tree stand. The two outer pieces were just about right, though a little heavy. We had reinforced the rungs with twine so I unwound some of that until we had enough to form a webbing of sorts between the two poles. I grabbed the buck's front feet and Brody grabbed the rear feet. Together we were able to swing him onto the sled.

I wrapped the whole mess with more twine. I didn't want it to fall off if we dropped the sled. It was hard enough getting him situated the first time. We gave it a test pull. Together we dragged the sled downhill for a hundred yards or so.

"Is this going to be doable?" I asked Brody.
"It's hard going but we can make it," she said. "It's all downhill from here."

It was indeed hard sledding. Rocks and downed logs impeded our progress. We couldn't decide if going around an obstacle or over it was preferable. We hit a root and both of us dropped our poles. We had to rest often, making progress even slower. Eventually, we tuckered out. We still had a quarter-mile to go, but we were beat. We sat and rested. All our water was long gone. I dunked my water bottle in the creek to fill it, offering it to Brody first. She drank half of it before giving it up.

We were still breathing hard and both of us were red in the face. The last part was the easiest but we didn't think we could make it. I wished we had an ATV down at the cabin. I thought of other possible ways to get our burden over the last part of the journey. Our neighbor, Richard, had a tractor. I thought it could make it to where we rested. I hoped he was home and willing to help, or at least lend us the machine.

I offered to stay with the deer while Brody went for help. A man is much more likely to be agreeable to a pretty woman than he is another man. It's one of life's basic truths. She was happy to continue on without me. She thought I might be bear bait sitting there alone with a dear carcass. I was still armed so I wasn't worried about a bear. She went on down the hill in search of a tractor.

It was almost dusk. It looked like I'd miss the after-hunt gathering with Banner and the boys. It would be a shame if they didn't see my kill. That was the whole point, but I couldn't think of anything that could be done about it. I'd bitten off more than I could chew. It wasn't the first time.

I heard the tractor fire up down below me and let out a sigh of relief. I simply didn't have the gumption required to drag the thing any further. I hated to admit it but age was taking its toll on me. There'd been a time when I could have dragged him all the way by myself. I wanted a cold beer and a hot shower.

I listened as the tractor made slow progress up the hill. The sun set behind the trees and Richard turned on his headlights. It took him almost an hour to slowly crawl up the steep terrain, but he made it. Brody was riding in the cab with him, looking tired.

"Looks like a nice one," Richard said. "Let's put him in the bucket."

I was glad to have his help rolling and tugging the dead deer off the sled and into the bucket. I could see Brody wasn't up for anymore heavy lifting. There was no room for another person in the cab of the tractor, so I rode down the hill in the bucket with my buck. I smelled of blood and deer guts but I didn't care.

Richard got us home and offered to hang the deer from the raised bucket until morning. I accepted. I'd had enough of Mr. Buck for that day. Just as we were tying him up, two sets of headlights came down McGuire Mountain Road and turned into our drive. It was Banner and company. They hopped out with beers in hand to inspect my trophy.

"Well I'll be a son-of-a-bitch," said Banner. "I figured you for a greenhorn. I thought you were blowing smoke about being a hunter."

Jake handed me a beer out of a cooler in the back of his truck.

"Pretty impressive," he said. "Congratulations."

All four men shook my hand and congratulated me. It made me feel proud, instead of guilty for killing.

"You boys have your fun," said Brody. "I'm going in to get cleaned up."

"That's a fine looking lady you got," said Rob. "You weren't fooling about that either."

"She's something else," I said. "Helped me drag this deer most of the way down."

"Might be two-hundred pounds," said Zane. "Long way down."

"He had some tractor help," said Banner.

"You think you could carry this thing down the mountain?" asked Jake.

"Maybe," Banner said. "I'd give her hell trying."

"You're younger and in better shape than me," I said. "I'm just glad we made it back, tractor or not."

I could see Banner studying me, trying to measure me. He was still suspicious. Maybe if I could kill that deer and get it back to the cabin, I was capable of removing Pop's body and snooping on the weed patch. His buddies kept feeding me beers and slapping me on the back. Banner didn't say anything if that's what he was thinking.

Fifteen

No one in Banner's group had seen a buck. They were all headed back out in the morning to try again. I needed to rebuild the deer stand Brody and I had dismantled, but wouldn't do it while the others were on the hunt. I told them I planned to take the day off and that I'd fix the stand on Sunday. Our little celebration broke up and the men drove back up the drive and out of sight.

"What did you think about Banner?" I asked Brody.

She had a knack for analyzing people, something she learned at the FBI. She could tell if someone was lying or acting out of the ordinary.

"His friends were all relaxed and having a good time," she said. "He was on his game the whole time, trying to figure you out."

"You think he knows that I know?"

"He suspects it, no doubt," she said. "But he can't confront you in front of his buddies. They seem to like you."

"Everybody likes Breeze," I said. "I'm a lovable guy."

"Banner isn't," she said. "He's aloof. Thinks he's better than the rest of us."

"His family has treated him that way," I said. "But I don't give a shit about his pedigree. A killer is a killer."

"So what do you do now that you've insinuated yourself into his inner circle?"

"I don't know yet," I admitted. "Look for some kind of opportunity. I'll think of something."

"Winging it again," she said. "Same old Breeze."

I was still struggling with a final solution to my mission. It was apparent that law enforcement would be no help, no matter how much evidence I presented them. Somehow, Brody and I would be the ones to take down Banner. I just didn't know how yet. The last thing I wanted to do was kill the man. I'd barely managed to recover from my last turn at dealing death. I was not a cold-blooded killer.

We spent the next day recuperating from our ordeal. I was resting with a good book when Brody turned on the SAT phone. There was a text from Bowdich. She called him immediately.

"Banner was suspected in a death investigation in Roan Mountain, Tennessee," he said. "A hunter's body was found, shot with a high caliber weapon."

"Not a murder investigation?" she asked. "Suspected but not a suspect?"

"Final report says accidental shooting," he said. "Shooter was never identified."

"So how does Banner's name come up?"

"Buried deep in a dusty file were some interview reports with other hunters and people close to the deceased," he said. "Several of them mentioned Banner but he was never brought in for questioning. No one asked about his weapon. Nothing tells us what caliber the bullet was. The whole thing was just written off as an accident and forgotten."

"How long ago was this?"

"Very soon after Banner's release from the military," he said. "We understand he may have some anger issues."

"You think?" she said. "The man's a killer David. Isn't there anything you can do?"

"I'm giving you new information," he said. "I ran your bullet. I've looked into this as far as I can. It's not an official case and I'm sticking my neck out here."

"Then I guess we'll have to take care of it the best we can," she said. "However we see fit."

"I didn't hear that," he said. "This conversation is over."

Whoever looked into the hunter's death in Roan Mountain didn't make much of an effort. Apparently, the senator's influence ran deep, even crossing state lines. Banner was untouchable. We could be certain that we'd get no help from official channels. I'd have to get my head on straight and take care of business, but I had Brody to consider.

"How do you think this is going to end?" I asked her.

"I'm afraid of how it will end," she said. "You've had tunnel vision since this whole thing started."

"I'm going to lay it out for you," I said. "Let's be honest with each other. I can forget all about Pop's murder. I can forget all about the dope. I can forget about Banner."

"No, you can't."

"If you want me to," I said. "If you don't want to see this thing through, and we know what's likely to happen, then I'll drop it. If we commit to justice here though, I'll need your help. I'll need your support."

"We can't let him get away with it," she said. "We know he's a killer. He could do it again. He probably will do it again."

"So do we do this?"

She put the phone down and paced the cabin floor. She didn't look at me for a few minutes. I watched her stand in front of a window and chew on her nails. She ran her hands through her hair and let out a big sigh.

"They're making us do this," she said. "The Sheriff, the FBI, everyone who's ever covered for Cody Banner. They are leaving us no choice."

"That's the way I see it," I agreed. "But I don't like it. I don't like it one bit."

"I want you to put that big brain of yours to good use," she said. "I want you to put that Zen thing to work too. Let's come up with a plan. Put that motherfucker down without anyone even knowing. Put this thing behind us. Fuck it. We'll leave this place behind if we have to, but we've got to end this."

That was it in a nutshell. Brody was of the same mind as me. We'd left all of our troubles behind, only to find new troubles here. A travesty of justice had been dropped in our lap. An innocent old man was gone for no reason. There was a foul air hanging over our little haven. Bad mojo was infecting the clean mountain air. No exorcist or voodoo doll was going to purify our atmosphere. It was up to us.

Banner was young and tough. He was good in the woods and no stranger to killing, but I had some qualities that he lacked. I could move like smoke. I could see, smell, and hear in another dimension. I'd made the mountain my friend. I was on the side of good. He was on the side of evil. I would prevail.

I spent days trying to plan out a way to force Banner's hand and catch him off guard in the woods. His friends had all taken off from work for the first week of hunting season. I couldn't have them on the mountain as witnesses. I didn't want any of them to get hurt either. I had to be patient.

Jake stopped by Friday afternoon to invite me to another cookout, even offering me a ride. I told him I'd be by later. I decided to play a little game with Banner and the boys. I put on my hunting gear along with a knife and pistol. I reached into our fireplace and used some ashes to blacken my face.

"What the hell are you doing?" asked Brody.

"I'm going to put on a little demonstration for Banner," I said. "Put the fear of Breeze in him."

"What can I do?" she said.

"Tonight is not the night," I said. "Not with his friends around. I'm just going to show him that I can get to him whenever I want to. Get in his head."

"Jesus, be careful."

I stood in the driveway and looked up at the night sky. I let the moonlight energize me. There wasn't time to go up and over the ridge. Instead, I walked west on Pigeon Roost Road until a bridge crossed over the creek. I slipped into the woods and acclimated myself to the lack of light. At first I tried to make good time, but eventually, I slowed. I'd never been in this part of the woods. I figured I could feel my way along until I heard Banner and his pals partying around the fire. They weren't expecting me. They didn't know I was coming through the woods, but I assumed stealth mode anyway.

Small openings in the canopy overhead allowed occasional light into the forest. The moon was up good and the sky was clear. Fall was strengthening its hold, chilling the night air. *Move like smoke, Breeze.* I crept up close to the hunting shack without being detected. The alcohol fueled conversation was in full force.

"Here we sit," said Jake. "Still hoping to get a deer. Breeze already got a monster."

"Beginner's luck," said Banner. "Something ain't quite right about that dude."

"You're just jealous," said Rob. "He bagged a trophy and he's probably home bagging his hot wife right now."

"While we're playing circle jerk around this fire," said Rob. "Toss me another beer will you?"

"His woman is a pretty little thing," said Zane. "He's either hung or rich."

"I wonder about that," said Banner. "Neither one of them goes to work. Where's the money come from? Nice cabin with some property. Something's up with him I'm telling you."

"Why don't you just ask him?" Jake said. "He's seems friendly enough."

"Before you all start a fan club, listen up," Banner said. "You see, I've got a little business up there on top of the ridge, in no man's land. Somebody has been poking around in it. It has to be Breeze, unless it's one of you three."

"We have no idea what you're talking about," Jake said.

I had crept in a little closer so I could see the four men. The three amigos were all looking confused by what Banner had told them. They obviously weren't part of it. He swept his gaze to each of them, scanning for any giveaways. Then he stood up.

"Fuck it, I gotta piss."

I saw my chance. He was headed around the back of the shack to take a leak. I stayed low but moved quickly and quietly. I got within fifteen yards of him and stopped, crouched right at the wood line. I let him do his business first. When he zipped up I was on him. He never heard me coming. I had my knife to his throat and an arm around him before he realized I was there. He tried to break free but I kicked the back of his knee, taking him down. The knife was still at his throat.

"What the fuck?" he yelled.

The rest of them came running. Once they saw me I pulled back the knife and offered my hand to Banner to help him up. He refused. I stood there grinning like I was having a blast.

"Woohoo," I exclaimed. "You shoulda seen the look on your face."

"Fuck you, Breeze," Banner said. "I oughta beat the snot out of you."

"I was just having a little fun," I said. "No harm done."

"Except for Cody's pride," said Zane. "How'd you let him sneak up on you like that?"

"I didn't figure my friends would do such a thing," Banner said.

"Don't let your feelings get all hurt," I said. "Go ahead and beat the snot out of me if you want to."

"Come on now," said Rob. "Let's all get another beer."

Banner gave me a death stare as we walked back to the fire pit. Jake tossed me a beer and gave me a nod of approval for putting Banner in his place.

"That was a bullshit move, Breeze," Banner said. "Don't pull nothing like that again."

"At least I let you take your leak first," I said. "Otherwise you'd have pissed your pants."

Jake, Rob, and Zane howled with laughter at Banner's expense. I gathered they weren't used to anyone challenging the big dog, but they liked it. My mission for the night was accomplished. I had two more beers and managed to sneak off without saying goodbye.

I'd exhibited some skills that should worry Banner. I'd certainly gotten under his skin.

Back at the cabin Brody and I made sure we were locked up tight. We loaded both rifles and both handguns and kept them at the ready. I didn't think Banner would try anything that night. He'd been drinking hard and suffered one humiliation already, but we decided to be prepared just in case. We'd stay prepared until this thing was over.

We heard several shots throughout the next day. Banner and his boys were taking deer, bucks or not. Later that afternoon Jake, Rob, and Zane pulled down the drive. They had three nice does in the bed of a truck.
"At least we got some meat to take home to our wives," said Jake.
"Where's Banner?" I asked.
"He's hanging up the buck he got today," he said. "Not as big as yours but a nice one."
"Sounds like everyone had a good day," I said.

Brody came out to exchange pleasantries with the boys. The last time they'd seen her, she was in hunting clothes and smattered with blood. This time she looked quite nice. Banner's friends were eyeing her like a shiny new pickup.

"Sorry to intrude, ma'am," said Jake. "We just stopped by to show off the fruits of our labors."

"Any time, fellows," she said politely.

"Mind if we drink a few beers?" he asked.

"Not as long as I can have one too," she said.

We were all standing around the tailgate drinking beer and swapping stories when Banner pulled down the drive. Zane tossed him a beer as soon as he got out of his truck.

"Heard you got a nice buck," I said.

"I think these three shooting up the hillside drove him out of hiding," he said. "Cold weather coming next week will get more of them moving."

"We'll be up there trying to get Brody a shot," I said. "Wear your orange, in case one of us gets trigger happy."

The veins in Banner's temples bulged and his face got red. I saw him clenching his fists at his side. He took a step towards me and pointed a finger in my face. He was trying to provoke me to throw a punch, but I didn't take the bait. I did not want to fight the man face to face. My prospects weren't good in a fair fight.

"I won't be challenged on my own damn mountain," he said. "Who do you think you are?"

"I own a good part of this mountain," I said. "My granddaddy didn't buy it for me either."

"Okay asshole, but I'm drawing the line," he said. "Don't step foot off of your own land. Don't track a deer onto my property or you'll pay the price."

"What are you going to do?" I asked. "Shoot me?"

"Go up into no man's land at your own risk too," he said. "I ain't playing around with you anymore."

"You've got no say over land that isn't yours," I said. "If I need to go up there, I will."

"You'll be making a big mistake," he said.

"Come on now, guys. Take it easy," said Jake. "The mountain is big enough for both of you."

"Breeze has just as much right as we do up above the ridge," said Rob.

"Shut up," Banner said, practically spitting. "Go on home. Take your meat and get out of here."

"This is our place," Brody said. "You men are welcome to stay as long as you want."

"I think we'll be getting along," said Jake. "You can't talk to him when he gets like this."

"Thanks for the beer," she said. "Don't be strangers."

The three of them piled into the truck, taking one more beer for the road. Banner did the same. Both trucks drove up the lane towards the blacktop road.

"That was rather unpleasant," Brody said. "You did a fine job of kicking the hornet's nest."

"You heard them," I said. "You can't talk to him when he gets like that. His temper gets the best of him. That's when he gets into trouble. He'll make a mistake. Do something stupid."

"I thought he was about to kick the crap out of you," she said.

"If we were at his place he probably would have," I said. "But I've been showing him that I'm not afraid of him, and this is my home turf."

"Toxic masculinity," she said. "I'll need to wash off all the testosterone."

"He'd walk all over me if I let him," I said. "You too. You see how the others defer to him."

"He's been the big dog around here for a long time," she said. "You know what they say. If you challenge the leader of the pack you better win."

"We need to stay on our toes," I said. "Be ready for anything."

"You still want to keep hunting?"

"If we don't go up there he'll know we're cowards," I said.

"One might call it good judgement," she replied. "Better part of valor and all that."

"One might," I said. "But I'm not. I won't back down now."

"So what's the plan?"

"I don't think his buddies will be back anytime soon," I said. "He'll be up there alone."

"We can't just track him down and kill him," she said.

"We can give him the opportunity to lose his cool," I said. "Tempt him into a tantrum. Use his anger against him."

"How exactly?"

"I'll know when I see it," I said. "One false move will give me justification."

"Justified," she said. "That's what we used to call a righteous shooting."

"To justify is to declare righteous, to make one right with God," I said. "Don't remember which chapter and verse that came from."

"Did you just quote scripture?" she asked.

"Best I could remember," I said. "It's been a long time since I went to church."

"I'm not sure killing Banner is something God would approve of," she said.

"Pop Sutton would approve," I said. "That will have to be good enough."

Sixteen

We rebuilt the deer stand below the plateau on Sunday. It was a lot of work just hiking up there and back. I thought we could hunker down in Pop's cave some nights to save us the trip, but Brody didn't like the idea one bit.

"We've got a nice cabin with all the comforts," she said. "It would be silly to sleep in the woods."

"Have it your way," I said. "Just trying to save you some effort."

"I'm getting much better at this shit," she said. "I'll hike back down gladly."

Both of us had gotten better at climbing. Our legs had strengthened considerably. We went up the mountain several days a week, trying to get Brody a buck. We didn't need the meat bad enough to kill a doe. The grocery store was only four miles away. The momma and her two yearlings had come back down the mountain and were feasting beneath our apple trees daily. If we were desperate for food, we could have shot them from the porch.

I tried to work with Brody on the ability to heighten her senses while in the woods. She'd always been aware, as a product of her training, but that something extra that I possessed eluded her. I think my time around Pop had made the difference. She'd never gotten to meet the mysterious mountain man. I was a total greenhorn when I stumbled onto him. He'd snuck up on me like it was child's play. I was embarrassed by how easily he'd bettered me in the woods, but it made me determined to learn his craft. Teaching it to Brody proved to be more of a challenge.

Soon it would be time to harvest the weed, and I didn't have any ideas on what to do about it. Banner was constantly on the mountain. He could cut them down and haul them out at any time. His friends didn't seem to know about them. Would he recruit them to help with the harvest? If I confronted the four of them, would they side with Banner? I was running out of time on that front.

I thought about harvesting the plants out from under him, just for spite. But what would I do with the crop? I didn't know anyone to sell it to. I didn't have those types of connections in North Carolina. It would, however, give me some satisfaction if I could keep it away from Banner. Once upon a time, I'd happened upon a good supply of dope down in Florida. I'd been able to donate it to a veteran's group that used it to treat chronic pain and PTSD. I could probably still get in touch with them if necessary, but that meant returning to Florida, something I was loathe to do. I brought the issue up with Brody.

"What about the sister?" she asked. "She has the connection. Just tell her to keep all the money this time."

"That's brilliant," I said. "Who is she and how do we get in touch?"

"I don't think Bowdich wants to help us on this anymore," she said. "Maybe just ask the Banner Elk PD?"

"I don't see what harm it will do," I said. "I'll tell them I have some of his belongings."

The police chief told us that Sky Sutton lived in a small cottage on the outskirts of Banner Elk. She made a meager living as an artist, attending all the local festivals and selling her wares out of her house. She had a sign on the door that read "Open when I'm here. Closed when I'm not." We paid her a visit.

"Sorry to bother you," I started. "But I'm a friend of your brothers."

"I doubt my brother had any friends," she said. "Popcorn Sutton's daughter is not a tourist attraction."

I had to put my foot in the door to keep her from closing it.

"I'm hardly a tourist," I said. "I knew your brother well."

Brody handed her the plastic tote with Pop's books in it, minus his journal.

"We know where he lived," I said. "And what he did for a living."

"Who are you?" she asked. "And what do you want from me?"

"My name is Breeze," I said. "This is Brody. We live up on McGuire Mountain."

"How do you know my brother?"

"I was hiking up above our property when he stuck a gun to my head," I said. "I accidentally stumbled upon his enterprise up there."

"What's that got to do with me?" she asked.

"It's about time to harvest his crop," I said. "We thought you may be interested."

"In what?" she asked. "Taking it to market for you? Pop's long dead."

"We want you to have it," Brody said. "We don't have any way to get rid of it. Be a shame to let it go to waste."

"What do you mean, you want me to have it?"

"We'll cut it down, and bag it up so you can come get it," I said. "You sell it and keep all the proceeds."

"Why would you do that?"

"Can we come in?" I asked. "There's more to tell you."

She let us enter and offered us a seat. She obviously didn't trust us, and I couldn't blame her. Brody tried to reassure her that we meant no harm.

"We are here to offer you help," she said. "Maybe in more ways than one."

"Why you want to help me?"

"We know who killed your brother," Brody said. "We plan to settle that score. Meanwhile, we have this crop that we want to keep away from his killer."

"Back up just a damn minute," she said. "If you know who killed him, why haven't you told the authorities?"

"We have," I said. "We've beaten our heads against a wall trying to get them to do something."

"It's Cody Banner, isn't it?" she said. "That boy ain't never been right in the head. I told my brother to watch out for him, but he didn't pay me any mind. He picked the wrong mountain to grow his weed on."

"Your intuition was right," Brody said. "We bought a place up there. Now we're going to take care of Banner."

"But first we want to get that pot to you," I said. "Before Banner can harvest it."

"Don't know that I want to be a part of crossing Cody Banner," she said. "My life is more valuable than a few grand worth of weed."

"If things work out right," I said. "Banner won't be a problem for you."

"If ifs and buts were candy and nuts," she said. "We'd all have a merry Christmas."

"I understand," I said. "You don't know us, but we're capable and we're trying to help you."

"Is your grandfather the grand poobah of western North Carolina?" she asked. "Is your daddy the godfather of Banner Elk?"

"We think our connections at the FBI will come in handy if necessary," I said. "If you don't want the dope then we'll burn it in the backyard."

"Let's not get hasty," she said. "You really think you can pull this off?"

"Wouldn't come here if we didn't," I said.

"Banner won't be looking for me?"

"No, he won't," I said. "You won't have any trouble. Make your deal and keep the money."

"Well this is an odd turn of events," she said. "Me and Marvin were never really close. Neither one of us was close to daddy, but I saw my brother in a dream just last night. He was holding out his hand to me, but I was afraid to take it. I dismissed it until just now."

"You're the only one that should benefit from Pop's crop," I told her. "It doesn't belong to Banner."

"Long as you can assure my safety," she said. "You call me when you got it bagged and ready to pick up."

She handed Brody a business card for Sky's Creations. We thanked her for her time and left.

"How are we going to get the weed down the mountain without Banner knowing about it?" Brody asked.

"Do it while he's at work," I said. "We know where he lives and what he drives. He can't stay up here hunting forever."

"What if he cuts it down before we get to it?"

"Then we take it from him," I said. "By whatever means necessary."

"Between the hunting rights and the weed, there's bound to be a confrontation somewhere along the line," she said. "That's what you're trying to set up."

"If he forces my hand, I won't pass up the opportunity."

"It's a dangerous game," she said.

"You still in?"

"Can't quit now."

We stalked the mountain every day, using Brody's buck quest as our excuse. Once she got settled in a stand I ventured off to track Banner's movements. If I didn't hear him or otherwise sense his presence I spied on his hunting shack. If the truck was there then so was he. He didn't know that I was keeping an eye on him. I moved like smoke, undetected through the forest. I heard him whether he coughed, sneezed or farted. I was the mist in the trees, a shadow behind a rock.

I checked on the pot plants almost daily, without leaving a trace. They were full of thick buds and ready to harvest. A cold front was on its way. They needed to be cut down before the first frost, but we couldn't risk taking them with Banner still around. We hadn't seen anything bigger than a button buck, but the does were plentiful. I debated whether or not Brody should go ahead and take a big female. Any reasonable hunter would want some meat in exchange for all that time on the mountain.

Banner was staying well away from our hunting grounds. He'd taken several does and dragged them back to his shack. The meat was more important to him than it was to us. When he was stalking a deer, he moved quietly or remained perfectly still, but he was loud and easy to tail when he carried his kill back down the mountain. I'd been all over his property in order to keep track of his movements. If he was aware of my presence, he didn't let on.

Several times I lined him up in my scope. I put the crosshairs on his chest and wondered if I could pull the trigger when the time came. It didn't feel right. He didn't deserve to live, but playing sniper gave me pause. I'd had to summon the will to kill that big buck. How was I going to shoot a man? I shook it off and continued my surveillance. I kept telling myself what a piece of shit this man was. I kept reminding myself that he'd killed my friend. I played an imaginary video of Pop going down after being shot, Banner, standing over his dead body afterward. I convinced myself that Brody and I had done everything within our power to get the police involved. As I watched him through the scope, I couldn't rightfully say whether I could pull the trigger or not. I'd decide when the moment of truth arrived.

I lowered the rifle and snuck back to meet Brody. A quick whistle let her know it was me. She acknowledged me with a nod. We met below her stand and spoke in whispers.
"No movement on the farm," she said. "Nothing but small does on the paths."
"Banner's skinning deer and drinking beer," I said. "I expect he'll leave soon to take his meat home or to a butcher."
"Are we ready to move on the crop?"
"We need bags and the machete," I said. "We'll have to work quickly once we start."
"Let's get ready in case he leaves tonight."

We stashed water bottles along our route back to the cabin. We'd travel light in order to handle the load. If we could each carry five or six plants per trip, we'd still have to go up and down a bunch of times. We were in for a marathon of mountain hiking. We also knew that stealing the plants could be the trigger that would set Banner off. Our feud was about to escalate.

We pulled some long burlap bags we'd bought at a local nursery out of the garage. The machete was new and sharp. We took off our heavy clothes to allow for more freedom of movement. Brody stood watch while I snuck down the road to check on Banner. His truck was still there. There was no movement outside the shack. It was too late to be up there hunting. I hoped he wasn't chopping down weed plants. I doubted he would do that in the dark though. He was probably just taking a nap.

I made my way back to Brody and reported what I had seen.
"We're on hold," she said. "Let's get some rest, see what tomorrow brings."

Seventeen

I snuck out at first light to check on the situation at Banner's place. His truck was gone. The beer cans were bagged up and there was a padlock on the door. He'd left the mountain. Now we had our chance. I hurried back to wake up Brody, but she was waiting for me with a cup of hot coffee. Waffles popped out of the toaster as I hugged her good morning. We ate quickly and prepared ourselves for the long day ahead.

"We've got a lot of work to do," I said. "But keep vigilant. We don't know when he'll come back."

"You think we can get the whole crop down here today?"

"It's asking a lot," I said. "We'll have to make the trip four or five times, depending on how much we can carry comfortably."

"What about Sky?"

"We'll stash it all for the night and call her in the morning," I said. "This is going to take all day."

"Here? In this cabin? Do you think that's a good idea?"

"In the woods close by," I said. "So far Banner hasn't trespassed on our land."

"A missing field of dope might change his mind," she said. "He'll know it was us."

"He can't exactly call the cops can he?"

"He could rat on us for possession," she countered.

"I hadn't thought of that," I said. "That would be smart, but I don't think he'll want to involve the police. He'll be livid and not thinking straight."

"You think he'll come here to confront us?"

"It's possible, but this is our turf," I said. "We outnumber him."

"So where's does it go down?"

"Up there," I said. "The mountain will decide."

"It's been building up to that all along, hasn't it?"

"It's my mountain," I said. "Pop passed it down to me. I've learned its ways and embraced them. Banner is a cancer on the landscape. It would still belong to Pop if he hadn't killed him."

"I hope you're right," she said. "I know you love it up there, but Banner has been around here for a long time. He probably feels like you're the cancer."

"I'll guess we'll find out whose claim is legitimate," I said. "The smart money is on me."

We climbed the mountain for the first time that day with a machete and some burlap bags. I had my hunting knife and we each carried a .40 cal Smith & Wesson. We were light on our feet and made steady progress. My gut told me that Banner was in Tennessee and that we were in the clear, at least for the day. We made it to the pot farm by mid-morning. I started felling the weed with the machete while Brody dragged the plants off and stuffed them into bags. I stopped and hefted a bag with three plants in it. It wasn't too heavy but it was awkward to carry. I had Brody load me up with another one. I could just carry two bags with three plants each. Any more and I would have trouble climbing downhill. Brody could manage two bags with just two plants each. One trip down the mountain meant ten plants transferred. We were looking at five trips.

I sniffed the air and listened to the sounds before we started down. There was nothing in our way. We scrambled down the slope at a good pace and hid our bags in some deep thicket just off to the side of our property. We grabbed a quick drink and headed back uphill. The second climb was only slightly tougher than the first, but it made me wonder how the last climb would feel. Brody trudged along like a real trooper.

The effort involved made it hard to stay in touch with the sights and sounds around us. I resorted to stopping occasionally to let my senses take in whatever information was available. I still felt that Banner was not on the mountain. We marched on. I cut and Brody bagged and together we made our way back down with our loads. We rested a little longer after the second trip and drank more water. We used the bathroom while we were close to the cabin. I grabbed a hand towel to wipe our sweat as we worked.

We had to rest again when we made it back up. My heart rate was high and we were both out of breath. We may have set an overly ambitious schedule for ourselves. It was well after noon and we were both starting to get tired. I chopped. She bagged. We took another brief respite before slowly dragging our asses back down to the cabin. Our pile of weed was getting large. We separated it into two piles and started another pile thirty yards away.

I'd like to say we were racing daylight, but we were hardly racing on our fourth trip. It was pure torture to our knees and hamstrings. My lower back was complaining loudly as well.
"I'm running out of gas, Breeze," Brody said.
"Me too," I admitted. "Stop for a minute."
I couldn't summon the Zen state that I needed to assure our safety. My breathing was labored and my heart beat equaled that of a Chihuahua on speed. Brody sat with her head between her legs, sweat dripping in a pool between her feet. We didn't move for twenty

minutes. I watched the sun angle lower in the sky while we recovered. Finally, we were able to move on.

I chopped down the remaining plants and helped Brody stuff them into the last of the bags. We couldn't carry the full load in one trip, but it gave us some extra time that didn't include hiking. I was in desperate need of a beer and some Ibuprofen. It was dinner time and we were both hungry. It didn't look like we'd finish before dark. I was worried that I hadn't been listening well enough. I'd lost touch with the vibrations of the mountain. Banner could be stalking us at that moment and I wouldn't know it. I hid my fears from Brody.

We got halfway down when Brody dropped her bags. She crumpled to her knees and looked to me for mercy. I knelt by her and wiped the sweat from her brow. I found a water bottle and let her drink what was left.
"I'm sorry," she said. "Just give me a minute."
"Wait here," I said. "I'm going back for the rest of it. I'll bring it back down to this spot. You rest."

"Be careful, Breeze."

"Stay alert," I said. "Take your pistol out of its holster until I get back."

I got back to the bags of dope and was suddenly mad at myself for leaving her alone. She was vulnerable and I was far away. I thought I was doing her a favor by letting her rest. Now I was afraid something would happen to her. I managed to hoist all the remaining weed and stumble down towards her resting place. By the time I reached her, I was in distress. I crumpled in a heap of weed and sweat by her side. The water was all gone. She offered to take what she could carry on down to the cabin, but I refused.

After too long of a break, I was able to continue. We left half of our packages there on the hillside. We stashed what we had with the rest of it and staggered into our cabin. I handed Brody a beer. I used mine to wash down three Advils and went in search of some whiskey. I'd learned to appreciate the painkilling properties of booze a long time ago.

We ate some leftovers heated in the microwave and zoned out in front of the TV. Some of the weed was still halfway up the mountain, but it would have to wait. My old joints wouldn't let me do any more climbing that day. Brody was asleep on the couch next to me. Before going to bed, I patrolled the house, locking up and looking out the windows. I laid Brody's pistol on the end table next to her. Mine was on the nightstand within easy reach.

He came for me in my dreams. I was staring down the barrel of his rifle and it got closer and closer until I was inside the business end of a high-powered weapon. Then it all went dark. Brody was shaking me awake. I was drenched in sweat and shaking with the chills.
"It's okay," she whispered. "I'm here. It's going to be all right."
I struggled to sit up and regain consciousness. Brody held me to her chest and rocked slightly back and forth like I was a newborn in his mother's arms. We had a history of this. Bad dreams had haunted me over the years, at different times and for different reasons. When I was awake, I could keep the demons

at bay. My mind worked overtime to block out the bad memories, but sometimes they found me in my sleep. Other times the nightmares were omens of things to come, warnings that I could heed. This one was telling me not to underestimate Cody Banner. Some bad shit was about to go down on that mountain, and I had best be prepared.

Brody climbed into bed next to me and we snuggled for a while, but I couldn't fall back to sleep. When I knew she was asleep, I slid out from under her arm and paced the cabin. I double-checked all the door and window locks. I hefted my pistol, asking it for security. It was four in the morning and I was wide awake. I got dressed and stepped out the back door to stare up at the night sky. Billions of stars looked back at me. Thin wisps of clouds moved in front of the moon then dissipated. The tops of the trees swayed ever so gently in the light breeze. I saw a pair of glowing eyes down by the creek, probably a raccoon.

Knowing that I had hours before Brody would wake up, I laced up my shoes and headed up the mountain in the dark towards the last of the weed. I could be back before she ever knew I was gone. The night air was easy to breathe, crisp and refreshing. As I left the cabin I activated my extra-sensory perception. It came to me quickly and naturally. The night lit up with sounds and smells. There was a talkative owl on the other side of the ridge. A possum was digging in the mud and moss for insects. The creek droned on as it always did and always will. Insects buzzed and twittered in the dark. The odor of raw earth was pungent like onions and garlic. Rot and decay complimented new life sprouting up wherever the sun penetrated the forest. It was glorious and almost overwhelming with its raw power to affect the senses. I took it all in and let it wash over me. I was a part of the woods. The mountain accepted my mortal presence and gifted me with its treasures. It cleansed me of my nightmare and gave me hope for what was to come.

I found the last bags of weed plants and slung them all over my shoulders. I'd been invigorated by the night's potions. I easily lugged it back down to the cabin. I had to go in and get a flashlight to locate the piles we'd hidden before adding the last of it to our stash. The job was done. We had all of Pop's crop secured in one location. Banner couldn't touch it now. Sky would reap the profits and maybe appreciate her brother's legacy. Pop would smile down upon us all.

I started the coffee maker and padded about the cabin on stocking feet, letting Brody sleep in. I took a cup out onto the porch to listen to the song of our mountain stream. There was a foggy mist descending down into the trees. Back on my boat, I always watched the sunrise over the water while the coffee helped start my day. At the cabin, the sun didn't make it above the trees until mid-morning. Instead, it trickled rays of light through the woods, bouncing off leaves and rocks under the fog.

I was on my second cup when Brody came out to say good morning. She did not look ready to tackle another exciting day. She was still worn out, hungry and a bit on the grumpy side. I made bacon and eggs as a peace offering. The toast popped out of the toaster, startling her.

"I already brought the rest of the weed down," I told her.

"I'll call Sky in a bit," she said. "After I wake up a little."

I was feeling much better and wanted to get started up the mountain to see what I could see, but Brody had not fully recovered. We still had to get rid of all that dope, so I stayed put, giving her time. She took a shower after breakfast and looked a little better. I didn't push her, but she finally picked up the SAT phone and called Pop's sister. Sky was eager to pick up the load. She was on her way. We gave her instructions on where to meet. The weed plants were piled up on someone else's property to the east of our cabin. There was a trail going up the hill to a corner on the blacktop road above. There was a small dirt and stone pull-off where folks could stop and take in the mountain scenery.

The trail was short but very steep. It went behind a neighboring cabin and came out on a gravel road that eventually joined the blacktop. I assumed the deer had beaten it down on the way to our apple trees. I had

Brody load me down with as many bags of weed as I could handle and started up the path. Brody followed behind me with a much lighter load.

Sky arrived on our second trip up the hill. She started loading her truck while we went back down for more. It didn't take us long to retrieve all of it. A heavy tarp covered the burlap bags. Four bricks on the corners held it down.

"I only have to make it ten miles," Sky said. "Most of it at thirty miles per hour. It will be okay."

"Best of luck to you," I said.

"Be careful," Brody said.

"Thank you both," she said. "I'm really touched that you'd do this for me."

"Thank your brother," I said. "This is the last of his legacy."

"It's more than I ever thought he'd leave," she said. "God rest his soul."

"Maybe it doesn't matter to you," I said. "But he was my friend. He helped me adjust to this place and to understand some things. I'm grateful to have known him."

"That's kind of you," she said. "I always believed he had a good heart. It was just impossible to bring it out of him."

"The same has been said of me," I told her. "But I'm trying harder these days."

"Bless you, Breeze and Brody," she said. "Now I've got to go."

We stood there and waved her off as she drove down the east side of McGuire Mountain towards Valle Crucis. Helping her was a bonus to our original mission, which was bringing the hammer of justice down on Cody Banner. I was anxious to survey the mountain and determine if he was back. Brody was more interested in a nap. We took the path back down through the woods and along the creek until we reached our cabin. Brody took her boots off and plopped down on the couch.

"I know you want to go up there," she said. "I just can't do it yet. Yesterday kicked my ass."

"Let me sneak over there and see if he's back," I said. "If he's not I'll come right home."

"What if he is back?"

"I'll want to track him," I said. "See if he finds that the pot is missing, or if he just goes hunting."

"I'll be here by myself," she said.

"If he's up on the mountain you don't have anything to worry about," I told her. "This is the safest place for you while he's up there."

"I'm so sorry, Breeze," she said. "I just need to rest some more."

"I'll probably be back in no time," I said. "If he's not back at his shack then we have time to rest."

"Be careful," she said. "Make sure your spidey senses are working."

"You sure you're going to be okay here alone?"

"I just need a few more hours of sleep," she said. "I'll lock you out when you leave."

I changed into my crusty hunting clothes. At the last minute, I decided to wear Pop's deerskin shoes. My rifle was ready as were my knife and pistol. I skipped the shower so that I wouldn't smell of soap and shampoo. I skirted the edge of the road until I crossed the creek. I disappeared into the woods and began the process of becoming one with nature. I noticed that dialing into the vibrations of the mountain gave me a certain happiness. I hadn't been all that happy during my time in Florida. I was either lonely or up to my nose in trouble most of the time. I loved the water and the mangroves and the beaches, but I don't think I truly appreciated them like I did the mountain.

I picked my way through the underbrush towards Banner's hunting shack. My ears and nose brought me data from far ahead. I slowed and made even more careful steps until I could see the sad little compound. Banner's truck was parked in its usual spot. I sat and waited and observed, listening for movement. He wasn't there. That meant he was up on the mountain somewhere. I didn't dare risk climbing the hill on his property. He'd have the advantage on his own turf. I had to backtrack until I could cross the creek.

I angled up and to the east until I was back on my own ground. I'd been over the same route so many times now that it was second nature. I could make good time and still maintain my situational awareness. Banner was not on the lower portion of the mountain. That much I knew. I pressed on, wanting to make contact so that I knew exactly where he was. Previously, I had always had the high ground and heard him coming. The roles were now reversed. I wanted to think that my superior skills as a woodsman would prevail, but I couldn't underestimate the man. The stakes were too high.

Where would he be? Was he simply hunting over on his side of the mountain? He'd already killed a freezer full. Would he head straight for the spot where the weed used to be? Was he here to harvest the plants? If he found the entire crop missing, he'd blow a gasket for sure, but what would he do? Would he immediately come looking for me? What if he went to the cabin? Brody was down there alone. I knew that she was capable of protecting herself, but she wasn't at top operating efficiency. The locks would stop him long enough for her to respond with a weapon.

I continued on my way, sampling the air for scents and sounds. I was three-quarters of the way up when something startled me. There was a new smell on the air, fresh and clean. I smelled soap and shampoo, maybe even deodorant. It was Brody. She was on the mountain alone. She hadn't stayed put in the relative safety of the cabin. I didn't have time to be upset with her. She was obviously coming to help, but she was putting herself in extreme danger. In her weakened state, she'd be no match for Banner. I was filled with fear for her safety. This crazy crusade was of my making. I'd laid claim to this mountain, but Brody was still learning its ways.

I tried desperately to identify any sound or smell of Banner but came up with nothing. I could see no signs of human activity, either from him or Brody. I knew I wasn't alone, so I crept onward, feeling the air for information that would lead me to one of them. My shoes were soft and quiet. My clothes smelled like the woods. I moved like smoke on a path to meet my destiny. Brody's scent grew stronger, but she was being extremely quiet. I was having a hard time zeroing in on her position.

I hoped that Banner would have the same problem.

I knew that I was closing in, but I was still uncertain. I thought I caught of whiff of gun oil, but that could be either one of them. Suddenly an unnatural whack rang out, like a bat hitting a ball. There was a crumpling of leaves and a grunt. Was it two bucks fighting it out? I froze in my tracks, begging for more information. Banner yelled out for the entire mountain to hear.

"I know you can hear me, Breeze," he yelled. "You want to come watch your women get fucked by a real man? Maybe you like that sort of thing."

I couldn't imagine that he'd moved in on Brody without me sensing his presence. It seemed impossible. Maybe it was a trap, but there he was, a little higher up towards the ridge. He'd managed to avoid being detected, but did he really have Brody? I had to move quickly, but I didn't want to give away my position in the process. I pictured the landscape ahead of me. Where would Brody likely go? How would he attack her without her seeing him coming? I kept moving and thinking as I went. She'd come up on the ridge near the tree stand on our side. If Banner was lying in wait, not moving, he could ambush her on her way to the pot farm. That had to be what happened. I kept moving and planning, my heart beating a mile a minute. The best vantage point was the rock that Banner had used to shoot Pop. The plateau was void of trees to block your line of sight.

I altered course to come up behind the big rock.

"Oh, she's even sweeter than I thought," said Banner. "This is gonna be a real bonus. You coming coward?"

There was no sound from Brody. I still didn't know if it was a trap. I moved as fast as I could without revealing my presence. I came up from the west and low-crawled to Banner's rock. I slid the barrel of my rifle onto a flat spot and looked through the scope. Brody was unconscious and Banner was on top of her. Her shirt had been ripped open and he was working on her pants. His own pants were already down, white ass exposed.

One side of Brody's face was bloated and red. She made no effort to resist. Her body was limp and lifeless.

"You thought you were going to show up here and piss on Cody Banner?" he yelled. "Who's the big dog now, Breeze? I hereby claim this piece of ass. When I'm done, I'm coming to fuck you too."

I put the crosshairs on his back. There was no moment of truth. This is what he'd done to my friend. I wouldn't allow him to take Brody. If I charged him with my fists, there was a good chance that I'd lose and he'd take Brody anyway. I had but one option. I didn't hesitate except to calm my breathing. There was no slowing my beating heart.

"God forgive me," I said. I calmly squeezed the trigger. Blam! Through the scope, I saw Banner go down in a heap. My aim had been perfect. A neat red hole appeared in the back of his jacket. From my experience with Pop, I knew what his chest would look like. He was still lying partially on top of Brody, with his face in the dirt.

I rose from behind the rock, racked another round into the chamber and collected my shell casing. I walked purposely but carefully towards the two of them. I used my foot to shove Banner's body off of Brody. He rolled onto his back, exposing the gore that I'd caused. Brody had his flesh and blood on her chest and face. She was still unresponsive. I wanted to break down and cry but there was work to be done. I had to get her medical attention. I had to make some attempt to cover my tracks as far as Banner's death. Saving Brody was of foremost importance, but I really didn't want to go to jail when this was all said and done.

I saw that she had the SAT phone clipped onto her belt. I barely knew how to use the thing, but I knew that Bowdich's number was programmed in. The Deputy Director of the FBI had made it clear that he was done helping us, but I hoped that he could summon help for Brody. I prayed that he cared enough to send her aid.

"It's gone down," I said. "Banner is dead. Brody is hurt real bad. We need a chopper up here to fly her out. Like now."

"Damn you, Breeze," he said. "I knew this would end badly."

"I'm not asking you to help me," I said. "But Brody is in a bad way. You will help her, won't you?"

"Stand by while we get a position on your phone," he said. "Can we land a chopper?"

"There's a flat spot just above our position," I said. "It's where the pot farm was. Otherwise, it's miles down the mountain. We don't have the time."

"Stand by," he said. "Stay with me."

A good minute passed until he spoke again. Brody still hadn't stirred. I was holding her head in my hands and attempting to clean her up when he finally responded.

"We've got your location," he said. "Help is on the way. The chopper is going to leave a team on the ground with you. Do what they say, you understand?"

"I'd rather go with Brody," I said.

"I appreciate that," he said. "But my men will take over the situation on the ground. They don't know the lay of the land. I need you to assist them so that they can assist you. Just do it, Breeze."

"I follow," I said. "You didn't have to do that for me."

"I'm doing it for Brody," he said. "But this is the last time. After this is done, we don't know either of you."

"Understood," I said. "My thanks. Tell that chopper pilot to hurry."

I cradled Brody's head in my lap and rocked her gently. I continually assured her that she would be okay. I used a bottle of water and a handkerchief to clean up her face. The red swelling was turning an angry purple. Dried blood caked in her hair near the temple. It looked like Banner had used the butt of his rifle to smash her in the side of the head. His body lay there cold and still, right next to us.

I scooped Brody up in my arms and carried her up onto the plateau. I didn't know how long it would take for a helicopter to arrive from D.C. or Langley or wherever it was leaving from. I took off my jacket and made a pillow for her head. I felt the urgent need to piss. I left Brody's side and walked back down to my victim's body. In the ultimate act of dominance, I soaked him with my urine.

"Fuck you, Cody Banner."

The mountain was mine, but it may have cost me the love of my life. It was a hollow victory. I was only there to make her happy. I'd given up the only life I'd ever known to come here with her and make a new life. If she didn't pull through, the mountain would only be a bad reminder of her demise. It would tell me every day how I'd let her die. I stood there waiting for the sound of a helicopter, contemplating how I'd kill myself if she didn't survive.

Eighteen

Several hours passed before I heard the first faint churning sounds of chopper blades. Brody stirred ever so slightly. I put my ear to her mouth to listen. It was so faint it should have been inaudible, but my ears heard her.
"I love you," she said. "I will always love you."
"I know baby," I said. "Hang in there for me. I love you so much it hurts. Shit's gonna work out. I promise. Shit will work out."

I stayed with Brody, down below the plateau, until the chopper landed. Six men piled out. I took them to Brody, and Banner's body. The dead man was placed in a body bag and Brody was carefully put on a stretcher.
"She'll be at Watauga Medical Center in Boone," the leader told me. "Cars are on the way to your house. These men will take care of things here."

I nodded in understanding. The chopper took off to the east, leaving me with four FBI agents whom I'd never met.

"Take us down to your cabin," a man said. "We'll follow with the body."

"What happens then?" I asked.

"You don't need to know the details," he said. "But it will be like this never happened."

"How soon can I leave for the hospital?"

"As soon as our cars arrive," he said. "They might beat us there."

"Let's go then," I said. "It's a long way, but it's not too bad going downhill."

The men took turns lugging Banner's dead weight down the mountain. I moved deliberately, tolerating their slow progress. Banner was dead, but all I could think about was Brody's welfare. She'd taken a mean hit to the head, not to mention the humiliation she'd suffered. The trek down seemed to take forever, but we made it to the cabin long before dark. Two big, black SUVs came down the drive soon after we arrived. The body was loaded, my escorts got in the cars, and they turned around and drove back out. I was alone.

I was desperate to get to the hospital, but I realized how bad I must have looked and smelled. I took a quick shower and changed into some decent, clean clothes before departing for Boone. I got a quick rundown from the attending doctor before being let in to see her. There was no skull fracture, but she'd suffered a concussion. She was conscious but was currently sleeping. I was told to let her sleep, but I could stay with her and talk to her when she woke.

I sat beside her bed and held her hand. She'd been cleaned up nicely. A soft ice pack rested on one side of her face, secured loosely with gauze. Other than a large nasty bruise and swelling, she was as lovely as ever. As I sat in the quiet room, fatigue overtook me. The adrenaline was gone and I was as tired as I'd ever been. I pulled another chair up to rest my feet on and dozed off at her bedside.

I replayed the shot in my dreams. Banner was in my crosshairs over and over again. I was at peace with what I'd done. His killing was justified. I shot him another dozen times. I never once wavered. Just to be sure, I replayed his killing of Pop Sutton. I saw him ravaging the woman I loved. Yes, I'd asked the Lord to forgive me, but I'd already forgiven myself.

Brody stirred just before daylight. I spoke to her softly in the dim light of the machines attached to her.

"It's okay, baby," I said. "You're going to be all right."

"Thank god you're here," she said. "I've missed you."

"How do you feel?"

"My head hurts," she said. "I'm terribly thirsty."

"I'll get some water and a nurse," I said.

The staff came in and checked her out. She was given a painkiller and plenty to drink. After they left, Brody had questions. She didn't remember everything that had happened.

"I shouldn't have gone up there alone," she said. "I was still so tired. I didn't stay aware. I was just walking in a stupor when a bomb went off in my head."

"Banner clubbed you with the butt of his rifle," I said. "Ambushed you."

"I thought I saw him lying beside me, but it's all a blur," she said.

"He's dead."

"I'm so sorry, Breeze," she said. "Are you okay?"

"Don't worry about me," I said. "I did what I had to do."

"It's your mountain now," she said. "It's all over."

"Mine and yours," I said. "Peace be upon us."

"Peace sounds nice."

I explained how she was transported to the hospital by an FBI helicopter. I told her what Bowdich had said about our future relationship with the Bureau. I told her about the cleanup crew that had accompanied the medics.

"Has law enforcement been here?" she asked.

"Nope," I told her. "Haven't heard a peep."

"David must have taken over the whole thing," she said. "The Sheriff won't like it, but there's not much he can do about it."

"I'm more worried about the Senator," I said. "He seems to pull all the strings."

"I suspect David will have gotten to him too," she said. "Turn on the TV. See if there's any news."

We watched the morning headlines before the broadcast was switched to a live feed from the statehouse in Raleigh. It was Senator Banner.

It is with deep regret and sadness that I report the death of my grandson, Cody Banner. There was a hunting accident in the mountains of western North Carolina that claimed his life too soon. We pray that he finds peace in the afterlife and absolution for his soul. The family asks that you respect our privacy during this trying time. Thank you all. No questions, please.

The FBI had used whatever leverage they had to silence the old man. If he was accepting this outcome, then law enforcement would follow. I expect some of them were relieved. There was no further need to worry about investigating the death of Pop Sutton. Justice had been brought to his killer. The weed had vanished. Nothing to see here. All was quiet on McGuire Mountain.

Nineteen

Soon I was able to bring Brody home to our quiet cabin in the woods. She recovered quickly and found an even greater appreciation for mountain living. She never asked about what Banner had done to her. I was content not to talk about it. She was a strong-willed and capable woman who was going to be just fine.

Eventually, she felt strong enough to do a little hiking. She wanted to return to the scene of Banner's death. I couldn't stop her so we went together. She showed no ill-effects from her ordeal on the way up. When we reached the spot she stopped and stood still. I watched her breath in the mountain air. Her nostrils flared as she took in the smells of the earth. I could tell she was listening intently to the sounds of nature and the babbling of the creek.

"I know what happened here," she said. "But that's behind me now. I won't let it continue to hurt me, or stand in the way of our life together."

"You're an amazing woman, Brody," I said. "I'm proud to share all of this with you."

"I'm sorry for what you had to do," she said. "But I'd have done the same."

"I know you would," I said. "We're a team."

"Now I want to come back up here with my rifle," she said. "I'm going to kill a big buck before the season ends."

"That's the spirit," I said.

It took a few days, but Brody got her buck. We cleaned the rifles and put them away. We hoped to never use them again. The doe and her yearlings were free to eat all the apples our trees could provide.

We settled in for the winter with a freezer full of venison, love in our hearts, and plenty of firewood. No one bothered us, not the police, not the FBI, and most certainly not Cody Banner.

Peace.

Author's Thoughts

Popcorn Sutton was a legendary Appalachian moonshiner and bootlegger. In 2009, he opted to commit suicide rather than go to jail. He did have a daughter named Sky, but as far as I know, he never had a son. There are several books and a movie about his life.
https://en.wikipedia.org/wiki/Popcorn_Sutton

My wife and I lived aboard our boat in Florida for almost eight years. Recently we moved to a log cabin in the mountains of western North Carolina. We are enjoying our new life in the High Country. For more details on how this life-changing decision was made, read my previous book,
Benevolent Breeze
https://amzn.to/2IeIjbL

There have been several psychological studies over the past few years linking proximity to nature with increased awareness and heightened senses. Exposure to nature increases energy and one's sense of well-being. "Nature is fuel for the soul."

I was busy splitting wood and preparing for winter when Hurricane Florence threatened to flood our little piece of paradise. The forecasts for the Blue Ridge Mountains were calling for up to a foot of rain. Our cabin sits beside a creek and we were worried. I accelerated my wood splitting schedule and moved all of it to higher ground. We readied our generator and took on supplies. The heavy rains never came. Nearby locations received up to six inches of rain, but we barely got an inch. The folks in the eastern part of the state didn't fare so well. We are thankful to have been spared. The irony is that we thought leaving Florida would make us immune to hurricanes.

*If you enjoyed this book, please leave a review at Amazon.

Acknowledgements

Proofreaders
Dave Calhoun
Jeanene Olson
Kai Rabenstein

Editor
John Corbin

Cover Design
https://ebooklaunch.com/

Interior Formatting
https://ebooklaunch.com/

OTHER BOOKS BY ED ROBINSON

Trawler Trash; Confessions of a Boat Bum
https://amzn.to/2DskT44

Following Breeze
https://amzn.to/2fXJgq2

Free Breeze
https://amzn.to/2fXILfv

Redeeming Breeze
https://amzn.to/2gbBjAx

Bahama Breeze
https://amzn.to/2fJiMe6

Cool Breeze
https://amzn.to/2weKg1l

True Breeze
https://amzn.to/2ws6Hzp

Ominous Breeze
https://amzn.to/2lPzg70

Restless Breeze
https://amzn.to/2Aicj0A

Enduring Breeze
https://amzn.to/2unav5I

Benevolent Breeze
https://amzn.to/2NCRA3f

NONFICTION BY ED ROBINSON

Leap of Faith; Quit Your Job and Live on a Boat
https://amzn.to/2NGxLYK

Poop, Booze, and Bikinis
https://amzn.to/2xCeqOj

The Untold Story of Kim
https://amzn.to/2QXoGce

Contact Ed Robinson at Kimandedrobinson@gmail.com

Ed's Blog: **https://creeksidemusings.com/**

Ed's Amazon Author Page: https://amzn.to/2N0AabO

Facebook: https://www.facebook.com/EdRobinsonAuthor/

Made in the USA
Middletown, DE
03 July 2025